OPEN SKIES
COOKBOOK

Jn 2023

Dear Pamy,

Be inspired as a family be
creativ. The great wishs vocal aisith
Ju will.

OPEN SKIES COOKBOOK

A WILD AMERICAN ROAD TRIP BY SARAH GLOVER

PHOTOGRAPHY BY KATRINA PARKER

PRESTEL

Munich • London • New York

AMERICA HAS ALWAYS HAD A PIECE OF MY HEART.

My connection to this land of opportunity runs deep on both a personal and professional level, and for some time now, I've felt the pull to return to this incredible land. I've lived here before. I've worked here before. I've road-tripped here for pleasure, and now I've come full circle with this profound opportunity to explore and create on a Wild American Road Trip. And I'm still overawed by its grandeur and natural beauty.

This place, this landscape, is wild. From humid subtropical South Florida to the granite cliffs of El Capitan, and beyond to the rugged rock formations and stark desert landscapes of Joshua Tree, the diversity of the landscape here is quite literally unreal. It's vast, it's sparse, it's steeped in history, and it forms the ultimate backdrop for our road trip and some truly great open sky cooking.

Growing up in Tasmania, Australia, every destination was a road trip away. Some of my fondest memories stem from when my brothers and I would rustle up some loose change for petrol and make a break for where the swell was best. Road trip meal-planning was minimal. If there was a jar of Vegemite, some butter and bread, or tomato sauce and hot dogs on hand, we were winning. The occasional roadside food stand and triumphant shot at foraging was just the cherry on top. The simplicity of those days gave me an appreciation I will hold onto forever, because to road trip with those you love the most was, and indeed still is, living.

One of the things that I love about travel is that wherever you go, food and culture intertwined is a language of its own. So as you set off to road trip America, I would really encourage you to educate yourself on the traditional custodians of the land, to pay homage to First Nations people at any given opportunity, try a indigenous inspired recipe perhaps, and above all else, count your blessings that you get to experience a taste of an incredible culture that came long before you ventured across this vast country.

From Native American cuisine (think indigenous and wild plants, animal ingredients, and cultivated plant ingredients) through to a traditional Texan BBQ, food represents a connection to place, and it opens the doors to the stories behind incredible people and incredible produce from all corners of the world. Food and culture also invoke nostalgia. So whether you're about to embark on your first road trip or your fiftieth, you can safely assume that the experience you're about to commence will take up a notable part of your reflective heart in years to come.

My love affair with America (and the birthplace of my said nostalgia for this country) started at sixteen when I ventured to the USA to work at a kid's summer camp in Virginia. There, the food mainly consisted of Sloppy Joes, big trays of brownies, and hot dog cookouts. While not totally inspiring, the food on offer was intriguing and a cultural experience which irrevocably invokes a reminiscence of sorts any time I think about the tradition of camp food.

When I was twenty-three, I spent a golden summer with friends on Amelia Island where the conversation around food, and the journey to buy produce was just as important as the meal itself. We ate seasonally, and ventured to roadside stands to buy peaches, peanuts, and watermelon every other day. When I think about Amelia Island in the summertime, my mind goes straight to a long bike ride in the heat, followed by a crisp, thirst-quenching giant watermelon on the porch. If I reflect on this time long enough, I can taste the sweetness of the fruit, and feel the camaraderie of my dear friends.

Over the years my ability to recognize what the road could offer grew. As I discovered my passion and calling, I became acutely aware of how the people you meet along the way, the places you visit, and the cultural element of food impacts every road trip experience.

Sometime between kids' summer camp in Virginia and summer in Amelia Island, I got my first car back home in Tasmania: a 1969 Volkswagen Beetle. While not totally practical for this girl and her surfboard, it did represent the beginning of a lifelong passion for character-infused vehicles that has stuck with me to this day. Ultimately, cars are an engine that will get you to various places, but they can also become a character in your life, another member of the family that ignites various emotions. From the luxe to the vintage, all cars have something different to offer, but what unites them, is that they all remain the most important element of any road trip.

Throughout our journey, I'll be accompanied by a number of different vehicles: one for each destination. While this speaks to my inner car enthusiast, when the opportunity arose to road trip with a unique collection of vehicles, this became the perfect way to round out my recipe and road trip offering. If you're traveling to the States from overseas, let it be known that there are loads of great car rental places over here, so have a bit of fun with whatever you decide to hire. Or, for those absolute adventure seekers, why not buy an old car for your road trip and sell it once you're done! I recently had my trusty Defender — "Harriet" — shipped from Australia to join me on my USA travels, and it's been incredible to have her on the journey over here with me. It feels like I have a piece of home with me.

So, with your car in check, here's my challenge to you. While you're prepping for your road trip, don't overpack. Instead trust that local ingredients will make your dish memorable in more ways than simply adding flavor. Connection to people and place while you're on the road is key to the best culinary experiences. Without packing your entire pantry, you may have to learn to forage, or spark up a conversation with the local barista around where to fish for trout, or buy great pork. And by doing this, not only will you learn something about the town you're visiting and the story of the producer behind your ingredients, but you're guaranteed to learn something about yourself when you sit in the company of the locals you meet along the way.

Practically speaking, there are a few things you can do to successfully plan your road trip cooking. Aside from taking this cookbook with you, keep your eyes peeled for a farmers' market, a butcher, a bakery, an apple tree in a field, a patch of wild blackberries, a flowing river where you can toss a line in, or a dairy stop when you're going through a town. Naturally, you can research purveyors that are off the beaten path but either way,

break your list down into protein, vegetables, dairy, pantry, and then foraging.

Simplicity is possible with great ingredients and when it comes to protein — the right cut, so I would urge you not to skimp on the quality of the produce you use. Always support farmers and producers — it's a must (both for the local economy and for the quality of the food you're purchasing). Where possible, cook over fire because that will give you another element of flavor. And remember that while you're on the road, time is your friend. The beauty in road trip cuisine is that you're generally outdoors, cooking in the environment that you've traveled so far from home to get to. So immerse yourself in it, allow yourself more time in the day to prepare, to try a new recipe and to break bread with those you've chosen to accompany you on your adventure.

There's nothing quite like a loose plan, a full tank of petrol and the prospect of a new location that awaits. So, dear traveler, as we gear up for your next road trip, let's prep your car, pack your pantry basics, and I'll show you some of the people and places that have influenced this book of road trip recipes.

It's good to be on the road together.

HOW TO USE THIS BOOK

Some of you may be about to embark on your first road trip, while others may be seasoned adventure seekers. Whether you're traveling to the States before you travel across it, or you're born and bred here in the US, these highlights will help while you're on the road.

First up, this book is designed to take with you on the road, to accompany you on your travels, and to inspire great food along the way. So don't be afraid to get it dirty! Just think, dusty pages will only reinforce all the good stories you're bound to come home with.

These recipes aren't finite to any particular state, so you don't have to follow them to the tee. While I've been fairly specific around certain proteins I have used throughout this book, what you choose to cook is entirely up to you, and the resources available to you in the area you're visiting.

Use this book to inspire, and remember to be playful with your cooking. No steak in the area? No problem. Go with what you can source! There are so many ways to learn from the state you're in, and that starts with produce.

Learn a little! I'd encourage a little education around food history while you're road tripping, remembering at all times to acknowledge the narrative of the landscape.

Fuel up! Don't get caught out, instead, take note of where your next gas station is (unless of course, you're driving an electric!).

Do a weather check! In Australia we don't have the weather extremities that are found in the States, so be sure to check for changes in the weather, to stay prepared along the way. While we're here, ensure you read the signs from the parks and wildlife, and always follow their protocol — there could be bears about!

Pack the right equipment! I'm fairly selective when it comes to packing pans and knives for open sky cooking. I use certain equipment for its versatility and durability, because, let's face it, we need to withstand the rough elements of the wild. While I would encourage you to pick your own equipment that works for your set up and budget, take note of the equipment I've used throughout this book. Hot tip! Two things I never leave behind when I'm camping are a portable propane cooker and a fire kit.

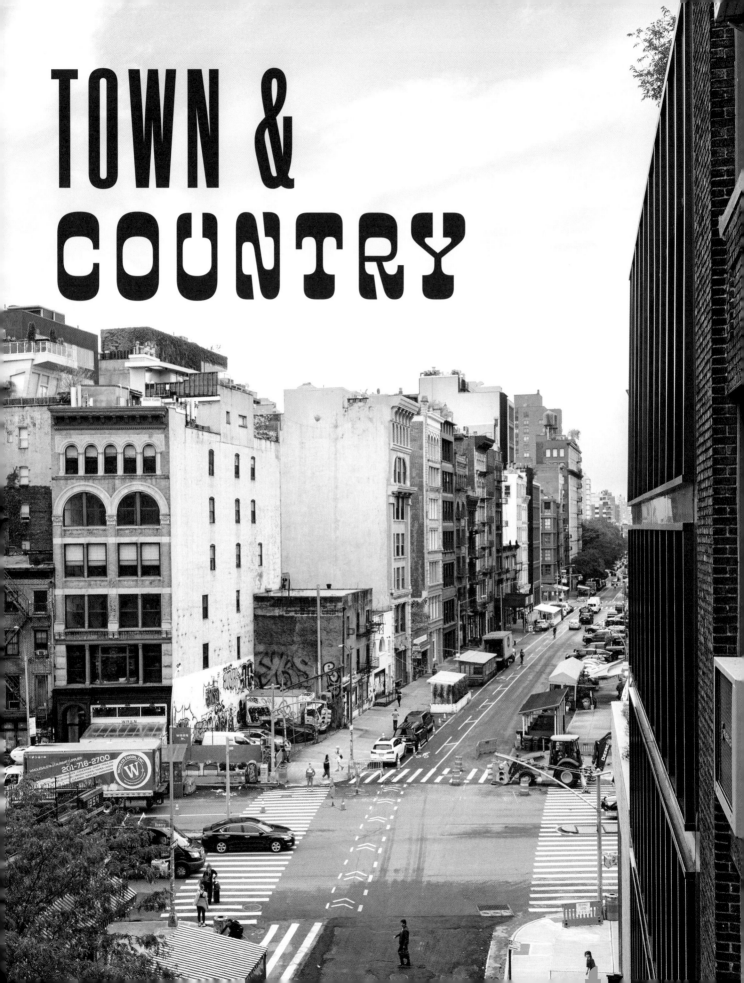

TOWN &
COUNTRY

UNFINISHED BUSINESS IN NEW YORK, UPSTATE & NEW ENGLAND

Ah New York, pivotal for my career. Parts of this incredible piece of land have been a big part of my formative chef years and my foundational adventure-seeker years, and gee, it's good to be back. It's not just the fantastic produce found at various farmers' markets in New York, or the unbelievable seafood found in Maine, it's the memory of those personal experiences I encountered when I hit the streets here for the first time many years ago; the energy felt at every intersection within this part of the States made an impact on who I was as a traveler then, and now here again today. Creatively, I fell in love with New York many years ago, and in a way, there's still unfinished business to attend to in this wonderful, wild city.

The first time I walked down Madison Avenue I was twenty-three and it was in that instant that I became enamored by this dream city. Out of nowhere, a lady shouted at me from across the street, "You look fantastic!" and I knew in that moment that NYC could instil a confidence unlike any other city, that anything goes — regardless of who you are or what you do — and that this was a place where I truly wanted to belong. That's the thing with travel: it gives you the opportunity to find new people, to experience new cultures, to take and glean and learn, and to then put those discoveries, those powers, right there into your pocket.

Once upon a time, I had a dream to run a cookie store here in the heart of the Big Apple. And I came close to making this my reality. I was making cookies from friends' apartments across the city and my business was moving along successfully for over two years before I invested in the oven, the cookie trays, and the dough machine. Then, after three short months of bricks-and-mortar trade, my business partnership failed. Essentially, the city churned and burned me, as it does to so many, and when I left all those years ago, I wasn't sure I'd ever be back. Many years later, a NYC-based publisher picked up my first cookbook, *Wild Adventures*, and I found myself back in familiar territory. I questioned whether a New York redemption was on the horizon. I mean, was this great city tossing me a bone?

From beyond the borders of Manhattan, across the rolling hills of the New England, over to the waves (or rather a dumping shore break) outside of the city, and into the icy cold waters from the snow in March, this area feels personal. I've spent birthdays in the Hamptons, hosted famils in the region, forged an incredible relationship with Martha Stewart at her holiday house in Maine, sampled wild blueberries at The Lost Kitchen (look it up, it's something else), dined with friends including Francis Mallman in Williamsburg, relished fantastic produce from upstate farmers' markets, purveyors and producers; and this is all quintessentially NYC isn't it? You just never know who might be in the camping lot next to you, or who might message you for a drink in the West Village, right? It's the magic of New York and its surroundings, and it always leaves you wanting more.

I guess if I'm being completely honest, coming back here, to a place that booted me out on my butt many years ago, feels a little exhilarating. A place that held so much of my formative chef years so tightly in its grips has now loosened its grasp and I can see all its beauty and wonder a little clearer, with a little more experience and a little less edge. Perhaps I had to learn from the city, rather than receive from this place. I had to discern from years of wisdom that the streets held and from the people who had made it here. Is it luck or is it grit? Could be both, but I think it's the latter.

Today I'm on the road here as an established chef, visiting and shooting in various locations that have inspired my career. And it feels good to show you what this area means to me personally. There's inspiration at every turn. For example, we shot Susan's Pie in Central Park, under the glory of the Bethesda Fountain, the Angel of the Waters statue watching from atop. The 1860s masterpiece was created by sculptor Emma Stebbin, the first woman to receive a public commission for a major work of art in New York City. Every time I stop in NYC, I visit this spot and take a moment to be thankful for all those people who came before me to blaze trails.

These recipes tell a personal story that is truly dear to my heart, and I dedicate these next pages to all that this place has taught me, to the travelers that have made it, and to all those who have not. Happy chef-ing, friends.

Brook's Brekkie Bowl

This recipe is from the café that I partnered with in Williamsburg in 2017. The dream was to make and sell cookies from the basement, on the side. Alas, the dream didn't really turn into reality, but I would never be doing what I am doing now if it had not been for this turn of events. I share this recipe in the hope that it becomes a morning staple for you, as it did for many of my NYC breakfast regulars at St. Balmain.

2 tablespoons coconut oil

2 garlic cloves

1 cup Tuscan (dinosaur) kale, leaves and stalks torn into bite-sized pieces

⅓ cup (60 g) cooked quinoa

4 slices halloumi cheese

2 soft-boiled or poached eggs (I like soft-boiled)

¼ lemon

This recipe is quite simple — the work is all in the prep and I recommend getting your ingredients ready so you don't have to stop and start.

Heat a skillet or cast-iron frying pan over medium heat.

Add 1 tablespoon of the coconut oil and the garlic and sauté for about 2 minutes, then add the kale and cook, stirring, for about 3 minutes, until the kale is a little crispy but not burnt. Toss in the quinoa and stir with a spatula until it's warmed through.

Move the mixture to one side of the pan, then add the remaining 1 tablespoon coconut oil to the empty side. Add the halloumi and cook for about 2 minutes, then flip it over and cook for an additional 2 minutes until golden brown (don't keep flipping the halloumi — you want to try and turn it only once so it stays golden).

Transfer the quinoa mixture to a plate and top with the golden halloumi. If using soft-boiled eggs, peel them, then add them to the pan and cook, tossing lightly, until they start to color. Serve alongside the quinoa and halloumi with the lemon for squeezing over.

<u>Breakfast & Brunch</u>

Feeds 1

Equipment: Cast-iron frying pan or skillet • Charcoal or gas barbecue grill (optional)

Seeded Honey

This is a lovely addition to your pantry when traveling. It's easy to make ahead of the trip, and you can use it in salads or add it to sweets and desserts. You can also pre-toast the seeds for a more nutty, savory flavor. Make sure you educate yourself on honey — try to find raw honey, with no added sugar or water — yes, believe it or not, some companies do this.

1 cup (250 ml) raw honey (plus extra if needed)

1 tablespoon sunflower seeds

1 tablespoon pepitas (pumpkin seeds)

1 tablespoon black sesame seeds

1 tablespoon sesame seeds

Half-fill a 10½-ounce (300 ml) glass jar with honey (if you need to adjust the amount of honey, please do).

Lightly toast the seeds in a frying pan over medium heat for 3 minutes until slightly fragrant. Spoon the toasted seeds over the honey, screw on the lid and turn the jar upside down — this will cause the seeds to infuse into the honey.

Set aside for a few hours, then turn the right way up. Serve with anything and everything.

Breakfast & Brunch

Feeds 1

BLT Bagel

In Australia, I grew up eating bacon, lettuce and tomato sandwiches. Recently, I devised this mash-up of two of my favorite foods: BLTs and toasted bagels with cream cheese. You must try this for your next brunch, perhaps with a blood orange Bellini on the side.

1 everything bagel, split

2 tablespoons cream cheese, softened

1 tablespoon mayonnaise

½ teaspoon dried parsley (optional)

Lettuce leaves of your choice

1 tomato, sliced

2 slices bacon, cooked to your liking

Toast the bagel to your liking.

Meanwhile, combine the cream cheese, mayonnaise, and dried parsley (if using) in a small bowl. Spread the mixture onto the cut sides of the toasted bagel.

Add the lettuce, tomato and bacon to one side of the bagel, then place the other half on top. Slice in half and enjoy!

Breakfast & Brunch   Feeds 1

Smoky Lobster Rolls

I was driving up the coast past Boston, with my friend Kat in a RV from Thor Motor Coach® RV, when I received a text from Martha Stewart inviting me to her house in Maine for dinner. I was a little shocked at the invite, but thrilled that we would connect again after first meeting in Tasmania, where I cooked for Martha and her family. She was very kindly returning the favor, and as we drove into Maine I saw lobster EVERYWHERE (which is unsurprising, as it's the best going around). Of course, Kat and I stopped to scoop up a lobster roll for a pre-dinner snack. Here is my twist on the classic.

Photo courtesy of THOR Industries.

2 fresh long red chiles

½ cup (125 ml) extra-virgin olive oil

2 live lobsters

2 garlic cloves, finely chopped

⅓ cup (75 g) whole-egg mayonnaise, plus extra for spreading

Finely grated zest and juice of 1 lemon and lime

2 stalks each fresh flat-leaf parsley, mint and chives, finely chopped

Sea salt and freshly ground black pepper

4 top-split, flat-sided hot dog buns ("New England" style)

4 lettuce leaves (I use Boston)

Sliced pickles, to serve

Light your fire and let it burn down for 1 hour until you obtain a medium heat (or use hardwood charcoal). While the fire is heating up, place a small cast-iron pot over the coals, add the chiles and let them char a little. Take the pan off the heat and set aside for 5 minutes. Add the oil and return the pan to a gentle heat for the chiles to infuse the oil for 1 hour.

Meanwhile, put your lobsters to sleep in a bucket of ice with a lid on it. This will take an hour or so.

Using a very sharp chef's knife, cleanly slice each lobster in half from head to tail. Brush the lobsters with some of the chili oil and place, flesh-side down, on the grill. Cook for 5 minutes, then flip them over and brush with more chili oil. Sprinkle with the garlic and cook for another 5 minutes, or until the flesh is opaque and just cooked through. Remove the lobsters from the heat and rest for 5 minutes.

Pull the lobster meat from the shells and place in a bowl. Add ¼ cup (100 g) of the mayonnaise, the lemon and lime zest and herbs and gently toss to coat (the lobster should be just lightly coated with the mayo). Add the remaining mayonnaise, if needed.

Taste the lobster salad. Some brands of mayonnaise have more tang than others; if the salad needs more brightness, add the lemon and lime juice. Season to taste with salt and pepper.

Spread some extra mayonnaise over the insides of the hot dog buns and grill for 1 to 2 minutes on each side or until toasted to your liking. Place a lettuce leaf in each bun, fill with a generous mound of lobster salad and pickles, and serve.

Rib-eye Steaks with Wasabi Bread Sauce

I launched my business, Bondi Bikkies, in 2018 in New York, selling cookies to cafés around the city. My dream was to make it BIG in the city. So I purchased some cooking equipment from my friend Ron who had recently closed up shop, and I was just waiting for the right space to come up, which ended up being a restaurant in Williamsburg. It was sadly short-lived. I returned to Williamsburg in 2019 to launch my book *Wild Adventure Cookbook*. As I stood under the bridge and served this dish, the meat was from my hometown in Tasmania, by Cape Grim Beef, I took a moment to pay tribute to my original dream and the new one that was birthed. Never underestimate a closed door. It could propel you into a new adventure!

4 rib-eye steaks

Sea salt

Wasabi bread sauce

3 cups (750 ml) milk

10 garlic cloves

1 shallot, diced

1 bay leaf

3 tablespoons (45 g) salted butter

3 tablespoons cream

3½ ounces (100 g) fresh bread (preferably sourdough; about 3 slices), roughly torn

Wasabi powder, to taste

To make the wasabi bread sauce, pour the milk into a saucepan, add the garlic cloves, shallot, and bay leaf and bring to the boil over medium heat. Remove from the heat and leave to stand for 1 hour.

Meanwhile, heat a charcoal barbecue for at least 30 to 60 minutes before you start to cook. You want the grill to be sizzling hot.

Strain the milk mixture and discard the solids, then return the milk to the pan and add the butter, cream and bread. Cook, stirring frequently, over medium heat for 15 minutes or until thickened, then blitz in a blender (or in the pan with a stick blender) to your preferred consistency. Add wasabi powder, to taste, then set aside and keep warm.

Season the rib-eye steaks on both sides with salt and cook on the grill for about 10 minutes each side for medium–rare (depending on their thickness), with an internal temperature of 130°F (54°C), or until cooked to your liking (I'm all about the medium–rare!). Remove the steaks from the grill and rest for 5 minutes before cutting into thick slices.

To serve, spread the wasabi bread sauce onto plates and top with the steaks.

<u>Main</u>

Feeds 4

Equipment: Charcoal barbecue grill
• Saucepan • Blender

New York Pizza

Cooked at a slightly lower temperature than its Neapolitan cousin, New York pizza is similarly steeped in history and just as tasty. There is such HYPE around NYC pizza! I thought the Italians made the good stuff, but the hype is real, and for me there is nothing better than a $2.50 pepperoni slice from a corner pizzeria in NYC after a late night hanging with friends. It's just so satisfying. I always add red chili flakes and extra Parmesan, but really, it's all about the tomato sauce base. Here is my go-to recipe — it's the perfect way to enjoy summer time in NYC parks with friends. After making the dough a day ahead and chilling it overnight, we baked these pizzas in a portable Gozney Roccbox portable pizza oven, but you can also cook them at home in your oven.

1 (14-ounce/400 g) can good-quality peeled plum tomatoes

Sea salt, to taste

Pizza dough

¼ cup plus 2 tablespoons (330 ml) warm water

2 teaspoons raw sugar

2 teaspoons active dried yeast

3⅓ cups (400 g) bread (strong) flour

1 tablespoon fine sea salt

2 tablespoons olive oil, plus extra for brushing

Toppings

Sliced pepperoni (optional)

10½ ounces (300 g) low-moisture mozzarella, half grated, half thinly sliced

To Serve

Chile oil

Dried red chili flakes

Grated Parmesan

Honey

Fresh oregano

To make the pizza dough, place the warm water in the bowl of a stand mixer and add the sugar. Stir to dissolve, then add the yeast, mixing it in with your fingers to help it dissolve. Attach the dough hook and turn the mixer to the lowest speed. With the mixer running, gradually add the flour, adding the salt about halfway through. Continue to mix for 7 minutes or until you have a soft dough.

Turn the mixer off, add the olive oil to the bowl, then cover with a clean tea towel and leave the dough to rest for 10 minutes.

Give the dough a final mix for 1 to 2 minutes to incorporate the oil, then transfer to a work surface, cover with an upturned bowl and leave to rest for 1 hour.

Brush your work surface lightly with olive oil, then divide the dough into three 8½-ounce (240 g) pieces and place them on the oiled surface. Shape each piece into a dough ball, then transfer to an airtight container and leave in the fridge for 24 hours.

>>

Main   Makes about 3 pizzas   Equipment: Gozney Roccbox portable pizza oven • Stand mixer

The next day, put the dough balls in resealable plastic bags and set off on your adventure.

Allow the dough balls to sit at room temperature for 1 to 2 hours before cooking (it's important to give the gluten time to relax, but how long this takes will depend on how hot or cold the environment is!).

The Roccbox needs to be fully saturated with heat with the flame turned to low — you may need to turn it up slightly in between pizzas to ensure the stone floor is at the desired temperature (about 350°F/180°C on the dial and 400–420°F/200–210°C on the stone floor).

Place the tomatoes in a bowl and season with salt, then lightly crush them with your hands.

Working with one ball of dough at a time, use your hands to stretch the dough into a round pizza base. Spread with a thin layer of the tomato sauce and top with a few slices of pepperoni (if using) and one-third of the grated and sliced mozzarella. Launch the pizza into your Roccbox and bake, rotating and turning frequently, for 3 to 5 minutes, until puffed up and bubbling.

Serve the pizza topped with chile oil, chili flakes and Parmesan, and repeat with the remaining dough, tomato sauce and toppings. I like a little honey and fresh oregano.

Elotes

Corn (sweetcorn) has an incredible history in America, but it can be hard to find anything other than the ubiquitous yellow corn sold in supermarkets. If you can, I recommend visiting a few farmers' markets and spending a few extra cents on heirloom varieties to experience the diversity of this amazing vegetable.

You will find this popular Mexican street food (also called Mexican street corn) on menus at many NYC Mexican restaurants and sold at street carts. I love eating it as a snack when traveling, or serving it as an accompaniment with other dishes, such as ribs, hot dogs or burgers.

½ cup (75 g) finely crumbled Cotija or feta, plus extra to serve

¼ cup (100 g) mayonnaise

¼ cup (115 g) sour cream or Mexican crema

¼ cup (15 g) finely chopped fresh cilantro (coriander) leaves and tender stems

½ teaspoon ancho or guajillo chile powder, plus extra to serve

1 garlic clove, finely minced (about 1 teaspoon)

4 ears of corn, husks and silks removed

1 lime, cut into wedges

The Roccbox needs to be fully saturated with heat with the flame turned to the desired temperature of 400°F (200°C). Alternatively, you can use a charcoal or gas barbecue grill.

Combine the cheese, mayonnaise, sour cream or crema, cilantro, chile powder and garlic in a large bowl. Stir until well combined, then set aside.

Add the corn to the hot barbecue or Roccbox and cook, rotating occasionally, for 5 to 7 minutes, until cooked through and charred in spots on all sides.

Transfer the corn to the bowl with the cheese mixture and use a large spoon to evenly coat the corn on all sides with the mixture. Transfer the coated corn to a serving plate, sprinkle with extra cheese and chile powder, and serve immediately with lime wedges for squeezing over.

<u>Side</u>

Feeds 4

Equipment: Gozney Roccbox
portable pizza oven, alternatively:
charcoal or gas barbecue grill

3 7

Mountain Trout

Trout from chilly mountain streams are at their best in late spring, when the ice has just melted. Cooks from Native American tribes make delicious meals using the entire fish, wasting nothing: the cheeks and eyes are considered a delicacy, as is the roe harvested from the females, which is prized for its distinctive flavor and its relationship to renewal. I made this by the rivers in the Catskills with my dear friend James Gop, where we harvested wild mushrooms and sumac. It was a beautiful afternoon and it felt right to pay homage to the land this way.

4 whole, head-on rainbow trout (about ¾ pound/360 g each), scaled and gutted, rinsed and patted dry

1 tablespoon ground sumac

Handful of wild fennel flowers, dried and pounded down (or use a handful of fennel seeds)

2 teaspoons flaked sea salt

⅓ cup (65 g) brown sugar

2 tablespoons extra virgin olive oil

Crème fraîche, to serve

Lemon wedges, to serve

Light a fire and let it burn down for 1 hour until you are left with hot coals and no flame. Place a grill grate 8 inches (20 cm) above the coals.

Open the trout fillets and fan them out like a book, to create an even, somewhat flat, surface.

In a small bowl, mix together the sumac, fennel, sugar and salt, then rub the mixture on both sides of the trout.

In the pictures James and I created a little stick-grilling contraption, as we wanted to keep it simple. But you can also just cook it on a grill grate, or a fish cage.

Place the fish, skin-side down, on the grill and cook for about 10 minutes, until pink and opaque with crispy skin. Don't overcook your fish. Trout can be eaten raw and is quite delicate, so you don't want to dry it out, but only cook until all the lovely oils come out and the sweetness of the fish adds to the flavor.

Transfer the trout, skin-side down, to a rock to serve. Dollop with some crème fraîche over the top of the flesh and season with salt and a wedge of lemon.

Main   Feeds 4   Equipment: Grill grate

Harvest Moon Mushrooms

In the fall, at the tail end of summer, mushrooms start to show up in the woods. I do suggest going with someone who knows how to identify mushrooms, and/or find a local farmers' market and buy some interesting varieties. I went foraging with James Gop in the Catskills, he knows the area well and is amazing at identifying mushrooms that we could add to our Mountain Trout. Mushrooms cooked on the fire can be creamy and add a beautiful, rich umami flavor to your dish.

1 cup (145 g) wild pine mushrooms (matsutake), sliced or torn into bite-sized pieces

1 cup (145 g) shiitake mushrooms, sliced or torn into bite-sized pieces

1 teaspoon fresh or dried Szechuan chile pepper

⅓ cup (80 g) salted butter

Salt

1 cup (250 ml) white wine, such as Riesling

Salt and freshly ground black pepper

Light your fire 30 minutes before you are ready to cook and let it burn down until you obtain a medium heat. You want nice, hot coals to cook these delights in.

Place the mushrooms and Szechuan chile in a large cast-iron frying pan with a good knob of butter and season well with salt. Place the pan on the coals and allow the butter to melt into the mushrooms.

Toss the mushrooms and add wine. Cook until the mushrooms have absorbed the liquid. You want the mushrooms to cook for about 20 to 30 minutes — pine mushrooms are quite fibrous and need to soften in the wine. Season to taste with salt and freshly ground black pepper.

<u>Side</u>   Feeds 6   Equipment: Cast-iron frying pan

Easy Veggie Fritters

Katrina and I hired a RV from our pals at Outdoorsy and hit the road in anticipation for some beautiful roadside feasts. This location didn't disappoint. In case you're over meat and fish, or, if you're anything like me, you have some unused veg in your cooler, these fritters make a welcome addition to any on-the-road menu, plus they're great for leftovers, too.

1 pound (450 g) carrots

1 pound (450 g) zucchini (courgettes), ends trimmed

1 tablespoon plus ¼ teaspoon sea salt, or to taste

¾ cup (200 g) plain Greek yogurt

1 teaspoon ground turmeric

½ cup (50 g) thinly sliced green onions (spring onions)

2 tablespoons chopped fresh cilantro (coriander)

2 tablespoons torn dill fronds

2 tablespoons thinly sliced mint leaves

Freshly ground black pepper

2 large eggs

⅓ cup (50 g) all-purpose (plain) flour, plus extra if needed

Extra-virgin olive oil, for frying

4 pounds (200 g) sliced halloumi cheese, if desired

4 lemon cheek to serve

Flaky sea salt, to serve

Grate the carrot and zucchini using the large holes of a box grater. Put the shredded vegetables in a colander and sprinkle with 2 teaspoons of the salt. Toss to coat and set aside until most of their water has been released, about 10 minutes.

Meanwhile, in a small bowl, whisk the yogurt, cilantro, dill, mint, turmeric, and the ¼ teaspoon salt. Taste and adjust the seasoning if necessary. Set the sauce aside for the flavor and yellow color to develop while you make the fritters.

Wring out the vegetables in a clean kitchen towel (that you don't mind staining orange) or a double layer of cheesecloth, or squeeze small handfuls at a time to extract as much moisture as possible, and put them in a large bowl. Add the green onions, remaining 1 teaspoon salt, and several grinds of black pepper.

Mix it all together with your hands, breaking up the compressed vegetables. Add the eggs and flour and mix with your hands until everything is evenly distributed. When you squeeze a small handful of the mixture, it should just hold together; if not, add more flour, 1 tablespoon at a time.

Warm a large cast-iron frying pan over medium–high heat. Pour in enough oil to heavily coat the base of the pan.

>>

Side   Feeds 4   Equipment: Box grater • Large
                                                            cast-iron frying pan

When the oil is shimmering hot, press a handful of the veggie mixture between your palms to make a 3-inch (7.5 cm) wide, flat pancake with frilly edges. Add it to the skillet. Repeat to make two or three more fritters and add them to the skillet without crowding the pan. Cook the fritters for 3 to 5 minutes, until the edges and bottoms are deeply browned and crisp. If the oil starts smoking or they seem to be browning too quickly, lower the heat to medium. Flip the fritters and continue frying on the other side for 3 to 5 minutes, until deeply browned.

Transfer the fritters to paper towels as they are done, and sprinkle them with flaky salt. Fry your halloumi one side at a time until golden brown, 2 minutes each side. Place on the side of the plate with your fitters. Spoon a dollop of the yellow yogurt sauce on each fritter, and serve with the remaining yogurt on the side.

Miso Charcoal Corn

Over thousands of years, Native Americans purposefully transformed maize through special cultivation techniques into the corn we know and love today. Maize was developed from a wild grass (teosinte) that originated in Central America about 7,000 years ago, although the ancestral kernels looked very different from today's corn. There are incredible heirloom varieties of corn found throughout America and I encourage you to look out for them on your travels as they add a wonderful complexity of flavor to this dish. This recipe is inspired by the one my mom would make me between school lessons, it was a household favorite. If eaten for breakfast, I serve mine on toast with a fried egg.

8 ears of corn, husks and silks removed

1½ cups (375 ml) heavy (double) cream

1 tablespoon white miso paste

3 tablespoons extra-virgin olive oil

6 eggs

6 slices of sourdough bread

Prepare a charcoal barbecue and allow the coals to burn down until they have a coating of white ash.

Place the shucked ears of corn on the grill and blister, turning occasionally, for about 15 minutes or until most of the kernels are dark brown and caramelized. You can also cook the corn in a frying pan or on a gas barbecue, you will just lose some of the smoky flavor.

When cool enough to handle, strip the roasted kernels from the corn cobs using a knife to run down either side of the husk. Place the corn kernels into a small Dutch oven, then use the tip of a spoon to scrape the pulp from the cobs into the pan as well.

Place the oven over the coals, pour in the cream and miso paste and cook, stirring occasionally, for 20 to 30 minutes, until the mixture is thick and creamy (if it struggles to get thick, add a little white flour to it).

While the corn and cream bubble away, place a cast-iron frying pan directly on the coals (or over high heat). Add the olive oil to the pan and fry the eggs. Toast the bread slices on the grill.

Divide the miso creamed corn among bowls and serve hot with eggs and toast.

Feeds 6

Equipment: Charcoal barbecue
grill • Small Dutch oven • Cast-iron
frying pan

Martha's Oat Caramel Slice

A dear friend introduced me to Martha Stewart's oat caramel slice, and it has been one of my go-to sweet delights for some time now. I asked Martha if it was okay for me to put this recipe in the book, as I'm just so obsessed with it. It's the perfect snack to take on a hike or a road trip: salty, sweet, with a little bit of choccy.

Vegetable oil cooking spray

48 soft caramel-candy cubes

½ cup (125 ml) heavy cream

2 cups (180 g) old-fashioned rolled oats

2 cups (240 g) all-purpose (plain) flour

1 cup (200 g) packed light-brown sugar

¾ teaspoon baking soda (bicarbonate of soda)

1 teaspoon sea salt

1⅓ (300 g) unsalted butter, chilled, chopped into small pieces

1 cup (170 g) semisweet chocolate chips

Preheat the oven to 350°F (180°C). Coat a 9 x 13 inch (23 x 33 cm) cake pan with cooking spray, then line with enough parchment (baking) paper to overhang the short sides by 2 inches (5 cm).

Place the caramels and cream in a small saucepan over medium heat and cook, stirring occasionally, for about 5 minutes, until the caramels are melted. Set aside to cool.

In a large bowl, stir together the oats, flour, brown sugar, baking soda and salt in a large bowl. Using a fork or your fingertips, blend the butter into the mixture until it resembles a coarse meal. Press half of the oat crumb mixture into the bottom of the prepared pan, then transfer to the oven and bake for about 20 minutes, until just set and starting to color around the edges. Cool in the pan on a wire rack for 5 minutes.

Sprinkle the base with the chocolate chips and drizzle with the caramel mixture. Top with the remaining oat crumb mixture and roughly flatten the top. Return the pan to the oven and bake for 20 to 25 minutes, until the slice is pale golden. Cool completely in the pan before cutting into squares.

It's unlikely that you'll have any leftovers, but if you do, the slice will keep in an airtight container for up to 1 week.

Feeds all your mates and their kids

Equipment: 9 x 13 inch (23 x 33 cm) cake pan • Saucepan

Susan's Pie

Susan, sweet Susan. I contemplated putting this recipe in my Florida chapter, but, you see, Susan is my NYC momma, and she is like no other woman. A poet, an advocate for truth, and a leader for women's voices. She also makes the world's best pies and, to be honest, even if you make this, it won't be perfect because it's not Susan making it. Feel free to make this your own by adding your favorite filling, and always do it with love.

Pie crust

- 5 cups (600 g) all-purpose (plain) flour, plus extra for dusting
- ½ cup (110 g) granulated sugar, plus extra for sprinkling
- ½ teaspoon sea salt
- 1 pound (1¾ cups/450 g) cold unsalted butter, chopped into tablespoon-sized chunks
- ½ cup (125 ml) ice water
- 2 tablespoons apple cider vinegar
- 1 egg
- 1 tablespoon whipping cream

Peach filling

- 10 peaches, peeled and cut into wedges
- ½ cup (110 g) granulated sugar
- ¼ cup (130 g) cornstarch (cornflour)
- 3 tablespoons freshly squeezed lemon juice
- 1 tablespoon lemon zest (optional)
- Pinch of sea salt

The easiest way to make the pie crust is to make two batches using a food processor. To do this, divide the pie crust ingredients in half, then add the flour, sugar and salt from one batch to the food processor and pulse to combine. Add half of the cold butter and pulse until the mixture resembles large breadcrumbs, then combine half of the iced water and vinegar in a jug and slowly drizzle it through the food processor tube while pulsing until the dough just comes together. If the mixture doesn't hold together when you squeeze a clump in your hand, add a little more water and pulse to combine. Repeat with the second batch of pie crust ingredients.

Transfer the dough to a pastry mat or a sheet of plastic wrap and knead each ball of dough 2 to 3 times, to help it come together. Gently flatten the dough into two 1-inch-thick (2.5 cm) discs, then separately cover with plastic wrap and transfer to the fridge for 30 minutes.

If making the pastry in one large batch by hand, combine the flour, sugar and salt in a large bowl, then cut in the cold butter until the mixture resembles large breadcrumbs. Slowly add the combined water and vinegar and gently mix just until the dough comes together. Form into a large disc, cover with plastic wrap and chill for 30 minutes.

Once your pie crust is chilled, remove one of the discs from the fridge and let it warm up on the counter for a few minutes (this helps to prevent the dough from cracking).

>>

On a lightly floured work surface, roll out the dough to a ¼-inch-thick (5 mm) circle, then carefully transfer to a large pie dish.

In a small bowl, lightly beat the egg and cream to make an egg wash. Set aside in the fridge until ready to use.

To make the filling, combine the peaches, sugar, cornstarch, lemon juice and zest, and salt in a large bowl. Transfer the filling to the prepared dish and smooth the top, then set aside in the fridge while you roll out the second piece of dough.

Preheat the oven to 425°F (220°C).

On a lightly floured work surface, roll out the second disc of dough to a ¼-inch-thick (5 mm) circle. Cut the dough into long strips — the width of the strips is totally up to you, but I do find that thicker strips are easier to work with.

To make the pie lattice, arrange the dough strips in rows across the top of your pie, then fold back every other strip and place a strip of pastry over the pie in the other direction. Unfold the strips over this piece of pastry, then fold back the remaining pastry strips and repeat this action. Continue until the lattice is complete.

Trim the excess pastry, then pinch together to seal the edge. Brush with the egg wash and sprinkle with granulated sugar.

Transfer to the oven and bake for 20 minutes, then reduce the temperature to 350°F (180°C), bake for an additional 50 minutes or until the pie is golden and bubbling. Allow to cool and enjoy with a little whipped cream.

New York Baked Cheesecake

I suggest making this cheesecake prior to your outdoor gathering or picnic. I know this means it's not really ADVENTURE food, but it's so lovely to serve this bright, refreshing cheesecake outside with friends. Very few people have the luxury of a backyard in NYC, making the local parks welcome green spaces that bring people together. This dish makes the perfect addition to a picnic on a gingham blanket, perhaps with a flask of tea or my Sweet Daisy Cocktail (see page 234).

6 tablespoons (90 g) unsalted butter, melted, plus extra at room temperature for greasing

15 graham crackers (each about 3 x 5 inches/7.5 x 12.5 cm), broken into pieces (or see page 182 for my homemade graham crackers)

⅓ cup (70 g) packed dark-brown sugar

1 teaspoon packed lemon zest, plus 1 tablespoon freshly squeezed lemon juice

1¼ teaspoons sea salt

2½ pounds (1.15 kg) cream cheese, at room temperature

1⅓ cups (300 g) granulated sugar

5 large eggs, at room temperature

1 cup (260 g) sour cream, at room temperature

1 teaspoon pure vanilla extract

Preheat the oven to 350°F (180°C). Assemble a 9-inch (24 cm) round springform pan with its base inverted, so the raised lip faces downwards. Grease the pan with butter and set aside.

Blitz the graham crackers in a food processor until ground. Add the melted butter, brown sugar, lemon zest, and ½ teaspoon of the salt, then pulse until the mixture resembles wet sand.

Press the mixture evenly into the bottom and halfway up the side of the prepared pan. Bake 12 to 15 minutes, until golden and set. Set aside to cool completely.

Reduce the oven temperature to 325°F (160°C).

Place the cream cheese in a stand mixer and beat on medium speed until smooth. Gradually add the granulated sugar and beat for 2 to 3 minutes, until light and fluffy. Beat in the lemon juice and remaining ¾ teaspoon of salt, then add the eggs, one at a time, beating well after each addition. Finally, beat in the sour cream and vanilla extract until smooth.

>>

Place the pan in the center of a large double layer of aluminum foil. Lift up the foil edges and wrap the foil tightly around the side of the pan, folding it under itself as needed until the foil is flush with the top of the pan (this prevents moisture from seeping in). Pour the filling into the pan (it should come almost to the top of the rim), and smooth the top with a small offset spatula.

Place the pan inside a roasting pan and transfer to the center rack of the oven. Carefully pour enough boiling water into the roasting pan to come halfway up the side of the cheesecake (this is safer than pouring it in and then transferring it to the oven). Bake for 1¾ to 2 hours, until the cheesecake is puffed and golden brown on top, but still slightly wobbly in the center (it will continue to cook as it cools).

Carefully remove the springform pan from the roasting pan, then transfer to a wire rack and leave to cool for 20 minutes. Remove the foil and run a small paring knife around the side of the cheesecake to help loosen it, then set aside to cool completely.

Unmold the cheesecake and serve.

HIGH GROUND & RUSHING RIVERS

NATURE'S FOOD HALL FROM YOSEMITE & UTAH TO THE NORTHWEST

It's not until you stand at the base of a giant sequoia, or face off with the grandeur of one of Yosemite's twenty mountains, that you can truly appreciate the landscape of this magnificent area. To capture it on camera just doesn't do it complete justice. And I can see why John Muir, one of America's most famous and influential naturalists and conservationists, and a man instrumental in getting legislation passed to better preserve Yosemite National Park, worked tirelessly to educate those that walked before us on the importance of experiencing and protecting natural heritage. He fought passionately to protect Yosemite and the Sierra Nevada in his time, once even taking President Theodore "Teddy" Roosevelt camping in Yosemite to show him firsthand why the area should be protected under federal law. And I get it. It's not hard to be inspired by this region. This most humbling of places is nothing short of spectacular.

Lying out at night under those giant sequoias was like lying in a temple built by no hand of man, temple grander than any human architect could by any possibility build.
— Theodore Roosevelt

But the antiquity of the area predates Muir by thousands of years. Steeped in Native American history, no lands are as spiritually significant to First Peoples as national parks like this one. Before the frenzy of the California Gold Rush reshaped the history of this area forever, Yosemite's Miwok tribes, for example, protected and preserved the natural cathedrals of the area, while the Washoe Indians tended and shaped the nearby landscape of Lake Tahoe. These are incredible places, worthy of deep respect and preservation, and the fact that we can visit these spots today and breathe in all their wonder and awe, fills me with gratitude, an appreciation for the First Peoples of the land, and an understanding of the historical significance of this area.

Only a ten-hour drive from Yosemite, the landscape in Utah — namely, Moab and Zion—is another world away. And that's the thing with America: the terrain, from one place to the next, is breathtaking. From enormous rivers and freshwater lakes, to stunning pine vistas, vast red rocks, carved canyons and desert as far as the eye can see, this region is truly wild. Until this road trip, I didn't fully comprehend the extent of water that flowed through the middle of this country. I really had to shift my mind to accommodate the concept of a land mass being filled with such an abundance of water. As an Australian, I understand the desert, but this is just a completely different experience in the US. The magnificence of life on the road strikes again!

Ahh travel, you go so far beyond the images I'd scoured on Google. I'm deeply grateful to have this opportunity to see a different type of geography, a collection of natural wonders in the wild. Wild adventure travelers, put this area on your itinerary.

Confit Tomatoes & Feta

I often like to pack in some quick and easy food ideas when I'm traveling, things that I know will give my dishes instant flavor. Confit tomatoes are fantastic for this, and they have a good shelf life, too. I suggest making this before hitting the road, but you can also make it over the fire.

Confit tomatoes

15 ounces (225 g) Roma tomatoes

5 whole garlic cloves, peeled

1 cup (250 ml) extra-virgin olive oil, plus extra for the toasts

1 teaspoon sea salt

½ teaspoon freshly ground black pepper

1 teaspoon kosher salt

½ teaspoon black pepper

Toasts

4 slices of sourdough bread (a loaf with olives or herbs would be nice, too)

½ cup (75 g) goat's feta

Grated zest of 1 lemon

Dried red chili flakes

I like to prep my tomatoes before my adventure, but you can make these while you're on the road too. Heat a cast-iron frying pan over a medium flame and add the tomatoes and garlic. Pour over the olive oil and season with salt and pepper. Cook for 30 to 45 minutes over a low heat until the tomatoes are soft and cooked through. Allow to cool completely if you're taking them on your adventure (alternatively, use right away.) Place the tomatoes in a jar and pack in your cooler for your trip or if you are on the road.

To make the toasts, heat up your grill (I used my Cadac portable grill with a grill plate attachment). Brush the bread with olive oil. When the grill is hot, add the bread and toast on both sides until golden brown. You can also reheat the confit tomatoes at this point, if necessary.

To assemble, spread a good amount of feta on each toast, then top with the warm confit tomatoes and their drippings. Grate lemon rind over the top and season with salt, pepper and chili flakes.

<u>Breakfast & Brunch</u>   Feeds 2   Equipment: Charcoal or gas barbecue grill • Cast-iron Dutch oven • Grater

Fire Fruits

It's not hard to find fruit when you're on the road and it's always a welcome bit of freshness. This recipe is also the perfect vehicle for fruit that is a little bruised or overripe. It's delicious for dessert and so good for breakfast added to oatmeal.

3 peaches, halved, stones removed (you could also use other stone fruit, such as nectarines or plums)

2 tablespoons extra-virgin olive oil

⅓ cup (75 g) coconut sugar or granulated sugar

Cream, for serving

Maple syrup, for serving

Light your portable gas stove. (Alternatively, you can use a charcoal or gas barbecue grill or even an open fire with a grill grate.) Place a medium frying pan on the gas cooker and allow it to heat up. Add the peach halves, cut-side down, drizzle in the olive oil and sprinkle the coconut sugar over the top. Cook for about 8 minutes or until the peaches are soft and slightly stewed.

Serve the peaches with cream and maple syrup or with your favorite breakfast porridge — for me, I love creamy buckwheat.

Miso Broccoli Breakfast

I'm such a fan of healthy, filling and warming breakfasts. I love the nutty flavor of the rice mixed with the miso dressing. You often don't get enough greens when you're camping and/or the ones you have tend to get a little beaten up. That's why I love frying them up on the cooker, you can add any other greens to this dish and fill your tummy up. It also works great for lunch or dinner!

Extra-virgin olive oil

1 cup (200 g) cooked brown rice

1 cup (85 g) broccoli florets

6 mushrooms

1 zucchini, cut into rounds about ½-inch thick (1.3 cm)

1 green bell pepper (green capsicum), cut into cubes

1 red onion, cut into cubes

1 avocado, halved

Grated zest of 1 lemon

2 cloves garlic, minced

Cilantro (coriander)

Parsley

1 fresh green chile sliced into discs

Bread of choice (I used a gluten-free seeded loaf), toasted

1 tablespoon miso dressing

Light your cooker (I used my Cadac portable grill with a grill plate attachment) and heat a frying pan or a flat grill plate.

Add the rice, lemon zest, garlic and about 1 tablespoon oil to the pan. Add the broccoli and cook until fragrant and golden. Transfer the rice and broccoli to a bowl.

Thread the mushrooms, zucchini, bell pepper and red onion onto 4 skewers, then grill the vegetable skewers until they reach the desired doneness. (I like mine al dente, so a little crunchy still.)

Divide the rice-broccoli mixture among 2 bowls and place the fresh herbs and avocado alongside the mixture in each bowl. Add a piece of toast to each bowl and top with 2 vegetable skewers.

Enjoy with some miso dressing zigzagged over the top.

<u>Breakfast & Brunch</u>   Feeds 2   Equipment: Portable gas stove
                                          • Frying pan or flat grill plate
                                          • 4 Skewers

Breakfast Cornbread with Wild Venison Sausage

While I was away with my friends from Kodiak Cakes, shooting some recipes in Moab and exploring, I was in awe of the sheer beauty of the red rocks surrounding me while I cooked. I felt like I was in a movie! I wanted to come up with an easy one-pan breakfast dish for my readers, so here it is. Feel free to adapt the cornbread filling to your liking.

1 tablespoon extra-virgin olive oil

10 ounces (1 cup/280 g) chopped wild venison sausage

2 garlic cloves, finely chopped

Handful of Tuscan (dinosaur) kale, shredded

1 (16.93-ounce/480 g) box Kodiak Cornbread Mix or another brand of your choice

Sea salt

4 large eggs

½ cup (112 g) grated three-cheese blend

⅓ cup (16 g) chopped chives

Salted butter, to serve

Hot sauce of your choice, to serve

Light a fire and let it burn down for 1 hour or until you obtain a medium heat. Set a tripod over the fire and attach a Dutch oven using a butcher's hook, so it's sitting 12 inches (30 cm) above the coals.

Add the extra-virgin olive oil to the Dutch oven, along with the venison sausage, and cook for 3 to 5 minutes, until lightly browned. Add the garlic and kale, and cook for 5 minutes or until the kale is starting to char.

Prepare the cornbread mix according to the package instructions. Season with salt, then pour the batter into the Dutch oven over the kale mixture. Make four indents in the batter and crack an egg into each one, then sprinkle over the cheese and the chives. Cover with the lid, shovel some coals on top and cook for 20 to 30 minutes, until the cornbread is cooked through.

Remove the Dutch oven from the tripod and leave to cool a little. Slice up the cornbread and serve with lashings of butter, a few splashes of hot sauce, and hot coffee.

Breakfast & Brunch   Feeds 4   Equipment: Tripod • Cast-iron
Dutch oven • Butcher's hook

Hung Steaks with Fire-roasted Vegetables & Farkleberry Dressing

Europeans introduced new plants and animals to the Americas, including bananas, wheat, sheep, and cows. Some Native American farming tribes, such as the Navajos and Mexican Indian tribes, began to cultivate these new crops and farm animals in addition to corn and other indigenous food. This recipe combines the more "modern" steak with farkleberries, a fruit native to North America, for a delicious result that is guaranteed to impress friends and family. Farkleberries are a type of wild blueberry that can be foraged in season, or use cultivated blueberries instead.

Steaks

4 T-bone steaks, untrimmed

Sea salt

4 cups/8 sticks (900 g) butter, melted

Vegetables

5 whole carrots, with tops attached

5 baby beets (beetroot), with tops attached

1 head of radicchio, leaves torn into bite-sized pieces

Shaved Parmesan, to serve

Dressing

⅓ cup (60 g) wild farkleberries (Native to America; you can use blueberries)

⅓ cup (80 ml) good-quality balsamic vinegar

⅓ cup (80 ml) extra-virgin olive oil

This is a simple dish, but it does require a little technique. First, light a fire and let it burn down for 1 hour or until you obtain a medium heat. Hang a tripod or crossbar 4 to 6 feet (1 to 2 m) above the coals.

Grab your T-bone steaks and secure a 3-foot (90 cm) length of string or garden wire to the top of each steak. The steaks need to be about 12 inches (30 cm) above the fire once attached to the tripod or crossbar. Hammer sea salt into the steaks, then tie to the end of butcher's hooks and hang from the tripod or crossbar.

Cook the steaks, rotating every 30 minutes and basting in the melted butter, for 1 to 2 hours, until the beef reaches an internal temperature of 130 to 140°F (55 to 60°C) for medium–rare, or until cooked to your liking. Remove the steaks from the fire and rest, covered, for 15 minutes.

To roast the vegetables, tie string or garden wire to the leafy ends of the vegetables, then suspend over the fire, next to the steaks. Cook for about 1 hour, until tender.

To make the dressing, place the berries, balsamic vinegar and olive oil in a small cast-iron pot and suspend or place over the fire. Cook for about 15 minutes, until reduced and syrupy.

Remove and discard the carrot and beet tops, then arrange the vegetables on a serving plate, along with the radicchio. Drizzle some of the dressing over the top and scatter with plenty of shaved Parmesan. Slice up the steaks, drizzle with the remaining dressing and serve with the vegetables.

Vegan Burger Taco

I'm amazed at the incredible accessibility to new products that support a vegan diet. Although I'm not vegan myself I do appreciate it and the wonderful flavors you can create with a little imagination. You're welcome to swap out the Impossible meat for ground beef (mince) if you like, but it's definitely worth a try before disregarding it.

1 (12-ounce/340 g) package Impossible plant-based beef

1 yellow onion, chopped

1 head of broccoli, cut into florets

2 cloves garlic, minced

1½ tablespoons salt

1 teaspoon ground cumin

6 medium soft flour tortillas

Garlic-chili oil

½ cup (120 g) crumbled queso fresco

Light your cooker (I used my Cadac portable grill with a grill plate attachment) to a medium heat. Add Impossible burger beef and cook until fully browned, about 10 minutes. Mix in the chopped onion, broccoli, minced garlic, salt and cumin. Cook and stir over medium heat until brown, about 5 minutes.

Warm flour tortillas over low heat until lightly toasted, about 30 seconds per side.

Assemble your tacos with the filling, serve with queso fresco and garlic-chili oil.

Nourish Ramen Bowl

I love a good bowl of goodness, sitting at the base of some of the grand stone cliffs in the Yosemite parks. I couldn't help but just want to look up the whole time with my jaw dropped. I felt this bowl was a great quick and easy meal to prep when wanting to just take it all in. Noodles are a staple on the road — this recipe offers an elevated way to enjoy them.

1 (4.58-ounce/130 g) package dried ramen noodles

Coconut oil

2 cloves garlic, crushed

1 cup (85 g) broccoli florets

½ cup (225 g) Impossible plant-based beef

½ cup (75 g) shiitake mushrooms

1 tablespoon tamari or soy sauce

1 tablespoon sesame oil

2 eggs

⅓ cup (18 g) roughly chopped fresh cilantro (coriander)

2 tablespoons sliced green onions

1 tablespoon chili crunch oil

Light your gas cooker and cook the ramen noodles according to the package instructions.

In a frying pan, add a teaspoon of coconut oil and the garlic. Add the broccoli to the pan and toss in the coconut oil. Continue to cook until golden in color. Transfer the broccoli mixture to a bowl and set aside.

Add more coconut oil to the pan and fry the veggie burger beef until fully browned. Add the mushrooms and continue cooking until golden in color. Remove from the heat and set aside.

Add the tamari and sesame oil to the drained noodles and toss to coat. Transfer the noodles to a bowl and add the broccoli and mushrooms.

Fry the eggs in the pan to your liking, then add to the bowl with the noodles and top with the cilantro, green onions and chili crunch oil.

<u>Main</u>

Makes enough for 2

Equipment: Portable gas stove or charcoal barbecue grill • Frying pan

Abalone & Chips

I grew up eating abalone. In California, you can't free dive for it, but I have found some great farmed abalone that tastes just like the ones I found out the front of my house in Tasmania. This recipe is easy but it's luxe.

- 2 abalone, cleaned and sliced thinly
- 3 tablespoons (40 g) butter, plus extra for spreading (optional)
- 2 cloves garlic, finely chopped
- Extra-virgin olive oil
- 1 pound (450 g) Russet potatoes, boiled to soft, thinly sliced
- Handful of chives, roughly chopped
- 1 lemon, cut into wedges
- Tartar sauce

Light your cooker (I used my Cadac portable grill with a grill plate attachment), and use a flat plate on top.

To prep your abalone, take it out of the shell and remove the guts and beak (I leave the frill on mine). Pound the abalone with a large rock to tenderize it, then slice as thinly as possible.

Heat a large cast-iron frying pan until it's smoking, then toss in the butter and abalone — it will sizzle! Remove from the heat, add the garlic and cook until the abalone starts to curl at the lip (about 3 to 5 minutes). Remove from the pan.

To cook your chips, add a good dollop of oil to the pan, fry the potatoes until golden in color (try not to turn them too much, as you want to get the sugar in the potatoes to caramelize). Sprinkle with the chopped chives and serve the abalone with lemon wedges and tartar sauce.

Main   Feeds 2   Equipment: Charcoal or gas
barbecue grill • Cast-iron frying pan

Bean Bowl

As we hiked to the top of the waterfall view overlooking Yosemite National Park, I had an amazing view of Half Dome and the valley below. When I hike, I look forward to stopping for a snack — it's like my reward for walking so far, and the added bonus is to stop and take in the joy of nature. Dehydrating meals has started to become a fun way to experiment with food, they provide nutrient-dense meals while traveling. I've even taken these on a flight before! True story.

1 (15-ounce/425 g) can mixed beans, such as black and kidney beans, drained and rinsed

1 cup (200 g) sliced tomato

½ cup (75 g) sliced red bell pepper (red capsicum)

½ cup (65 g) diced carrot

2 tablespoons smoked paprika

½ teaspoon ground cumin

½ teaspoon garlic powder

½ teaspoon chipotle powder

½ ají molido chile powder

Preheat your dehydrator to 140°F (60°C).

On a tray from your dehydrator, add the beans in an even layer. Slide them in the dehydrator, then repeat this step for the tomatoes, pepper, and carrots, making sure that they are arranged in even layers so they will dehydrate evenly.

Once the beans and vegetables are dehydrated, after about 7 hours, they should be stiff and dry, not moist to the touch.

Place the dehydrated beans and vegetables in a bowl, add the spices and salt, and mix to combine. Transfer the mixture to resealable plastic bags or reusable silicone bags. This will make enough for two meals.

To rehydrate, boil 2 cups (500 ml) of water in your jet boil, and add the mix. Allow to sit for 10 minutes, stirring again as needed, and heat again if you wish. These are extra yummy with a dollop of sour cream and cheese.

Campfire Breadsticks

We made this while camping in Moab with my friends from Kodiak Cakes. It felt very primal to make bread dough in the dirt, and cook it over the fire. I have a new level of appreciation for how they used to cook without much back in the day. No running water, no gas cook tops, just basics. This recipe is so fun to make with your friends, and adding some cheese to the breadsticks makes for a memorable meal. Serve these breadsticks as a starter or alongside a main course.

2 cups (240 g) bread flour

2 teaspoons active dried yeast

1 teaspoon sea salt

1 cup (250 ml) warm water (use seawater if you're by the ocean)

1½ cups (375 ml) extra-virgin olive oil

½ garlic bulb

Grated cheese of your choice (I like blue cheese and Manchego)

Light a fire and let it burn down for 1 hour or until you obtain a medium heat.

Meanwhile, in a large bowl, combine the bread flour, yeast and salt. Add the warm water and ½ cup (125 ml) of the olive oil and form the mixture into a shaggy dough. Knead the dough for 5 to 8 minutes, until smooth and elastic.

Cover the bowl with a tea towel and set aside in a warm place for 1 hour, or until the dough is doubled in size.

Meanwhile, place the garlic and the remaining 1 cup (250 ml) olive oil in a heatproof bowl and place it by the fire to warm through. This will infuse the oil with the garlic.

Divide the dough into eight pieces, then roll each piece into a 10-inch (25 cm) long rope. Brush the dough ropes with the garlic oil, then wrap each rope around the end of a long roasting stick, pressing the ends of the dough onto the sticks to secure.

Hold or prop the sticks over the hot coals for about 10 minutes, rotating until the breadsticks are cooked through and golden.

Allow the breadsticks to cool for 5 minutes, then slide off the sticks and serve with cheese.

Makes 8

Equipment: Fire pit • 10 long sticks

Fire Cheeses

This recipe has become a staple at all the campouts and events I do. It's simple and just so delicious, and makes a perfect starter to any meal. It's also fun to try to find a creamery when on the road — to make the campfire story around this dish even more interesting.

8 ounces (250 g) blue cheese

1 (8-ounce/250 g) round of Brie or Camembert

Manchego cheese or a hard cheddar-style cheese that will melt

3 sprigs of fresh thyme

Honeycomb

1 batch of my Campfire Breadsticks (see page 98), for serving

Light your fire 30 minutes before you are ready to cook and let it burn down until you obtain a low heat.

Place a cast-iron chargrill pan on the fire so it gets nice and hot (you can also use a cast-iron frying pan).

Add the cheeses and the thyme sprigs and cook until golden and starting to melt. Flip all of them once.

Once the cheeses are melty, add the honeycomb to the top and serve with grilled bread.

Side

Feeds 4

Equipment: Cast-iron chargrill
or frying pan

Apple-stuffed Blueberry & Corn "Muffins"

These "muffins" are fun to make with family and friends, the kids can get involved too. Just allow a little extra-time to teach the little ones the way, and I guarantee it will taste that much sweeter when you eat it. I made them while camping in Utah with my pals from Kodiak Cakes and we had a lot of fun exploring the area on this trip. And here's a little camp hack to make it easy: buy a box of Kodiak blueberry cake mix and opt out of the mixture below.

4 Granny Smith apples

1 cup (165 g) blueberries, plus extra to serve

1 cup (138 g) cornmeal

1 cup (120 g) all-purpose (plain) flour

⅓ cup (80 g) granulated sugar

2 teaspoons baking powder

½ teaspoon sea salt

1 large egg, beaten

¼ cup (60 ml) canola oil

1 cup (250 ml) milk

Zest of 1 lemon

Salted butter at room temperature, to serve

Light a fire and let it burn down for 1 hour or until you obtain a medium heat.

Slice the tops off the apples and set aside. Using a corer, core the apples three-quarters of the way through, but keep the bases intact. Scoop out most of the apple flesh and roughly chop.

In a large bowl, mix together the blueberries, cornmeal, flour, sugar, baking powder and salt. Add the egg, oil and milk and stir gently to combine. Finally, add the apple and lemon zest, and stir through. Spoon the batter into the hollowed-out apples and place the apple lids on top. Wrap the apples in aluminum foil.

Use a shovel to make space among the coals away from the center of the fire. Add the apples, shovel some coals on top and cook for 15 to 20 minutes, until soft.

Unwrap the apples and serve with soft butter and a few extra blueberries.

Feeds 4

Equipment: Fire pit or charcoal
barbecue grill • Corer

SURFING
THE
WEST COAST

DIVE RIGHT INTO BIG SUR & SAN DIEGO VIA MALIBU

I'm intrigued by the West Coast of America, and I was even before we set off on this incredible wild road trip. You see, before getting here I'd sort of boxed California into this preconceived notion I had in my head. Maybe because it always felt a little familiar (cue Australia's coastal living, surf vibe and cold Tasmania-type water), or maybe it was because I'd already spent a little bit of time here and thought I understood the region. The truth is, when dealing with every type of landscape from the Big Sur Redwood Forest to the coast of San Jose, I didn't really know the Golden State. And that's what really excited me because when I got here, I felt like a newbie to the area. California felt like a true adventure to be uncovered.

My first stateside road trip — an absolute right of passage — was in California some six years ago. Armed with my first cookbook (which I was promoting at the time), a 1960s Ford pickup truck named "Blanca," and some of my friends in tow, we cruised up the coast, sharing the good news of my wild adventures. I remember feeling immediately

struck by the sense of community, the warmth of the people, the diversity of the culture, the landscape, and the incredible vibes from Californian people. While I've taken up residence on the West Coast for now, and I'm living out the Californian surf dream, when I set out to rediscover the area for this Wild American Road Trip, I really longed to embrace those feelings again, and California didn't disappoint. Australians think we have our beach culture tapped (and we do of course; a summer Down Under is something to write home about), but Californians — well, Californians know how to do it right, too.

Underdeveloped and still thriving with surf culture, the beaches in California have dark sand, they're rocky in part, and the water is so cold it can challenge your orientation when you consider that the desert's on your doorstep. Shouldn't the water feel warm? (Spoiler: it doesn't.) With diverse characters and cars at every turn, there's a familiarity here that does remind me of my childhood, and it's a feeling that catches me out every now and then. Contrary to the idea of discovery around travel, I often find we innately look for a bit of home wherever we go (I always try to spot the Australian in the lineup!), and that familiarity in California feels good, if you know what I mean.

While this region oozes beach culture, this state does have more than surfing to offer. There's a reason it's so heavily populated. There is so much on offer here; with an array of national parks you can be camping seaside in the morning and snowboarding in Tahoe in the afternoon. But it's also about the food offering.

One of the other things I love about California is the produce. As the largest producer of food in the USA despite having less than 4 percent of the farms in the country, the Golden State also grows an abundance of acorns, mushrooms, flowering plants, berries, nuts, stems and roots, prickly pear, wild cherries, manzanita berries, in addition to cultivated lime trees, orange trees, and peppercorn

trees. All this citrus this close to the desert? This place is remarkable. Oh, and remember the cold water I referred to earlier? It's great for anglers interested in fishing, too.

When it comes to open-fire cooking, things work differently in California. With strict fire restrictions currently in place, some municipalities in the state have placed incredible charcoal barbecue grills at many beaches which adhere to their environmental and fire safety regulations. Naturally, this will have an impact on some of the recipes you can create, which is another reason I'm so excited to show you what this state means to me and the recipes that you can use while you're in the area. Word to the wise: it's good to have lump wood charcoal on hand for this leg of the journey, as you never know when you're going to see one of those beach grill setups. Of course, given the fire restrictions, I'd suggest carrying a propane gas grill with you, too.

For now though, it's time to enjoy those California sunset vibes.

Sweetcorn Bagels

There are so many ways to enjoy fresh corn (we call it "sweetcorn" in Australia) — it's such a versatile and easy-to-cook vegetable. I didn't grow up eating a lot of it, but it is hugely popular in the United States. (Corn is native to the Americas and was the staple grain of indigenous Americans.) I'm a big fan of pairing it with miso as it adds a lovely complex flavor. This dish can be made out of your camper, on the top of a mountain or around the campfire.

3 tablespoons extra-virgin olive oil, divided

2 ears of corn, kernels stripped

2 garlic cloves, finely chopped

1 teaspoon white miso

Handful of kale leaves, shredded

5 green onions (spring onions), thinly sliced

4 eggs

4 good-quality bagels, split

Sliced triple cream Brie

Heat 1 tablespoon of the olive oil in a cast-iron frying pan over medium–high heat. Add the corn kernels and cook for 5 minutes, until they start to turn bright yellow and pop a little. Add the garlic, miso, kale and green onions, and continue to cook for another 3 minutes or until the kale is wilted and bright green.

Using a wooden spoon, make four small wells in the corn mixture, each large enough to hold an egg. Crack the eggs into the wells and fry for about 3 minutes, until the whites are just set and the yolks are cooked to your liking.

Meanwhile, heat the remaining 2 tablespoons olive oil in a separate frying pan over medium–high heat. Add the bagels, cut-side down, and toast to your liking.

To serve, place slices of triple cream Brie on the bottom half of each bagel. Roughly divide the corn-and-egg mixture into quarters, making sure that each quarter has an egg. Divide among the bagels and close with the bagel tops.

Feeds 4

Equipment: Gas burner
• 2 cast-iron frying pans

Easy Road Trip Focaccia

In October 2021, I went on a trip with THOR Industries. We found a little bakery in Newport Beach selling fresh pizza dough in what looked like ice cream tubs. I instantly knew this would come in handy and bought some. As we drove up the coast through Big Sur, en route to the Napa Valley, it was nearing dinnertime and the sun was setting. We whipped the vehicle off the road and found a scenic spot to make an easy dinner. This is the dish I created. Like most of the recipes I come up with, it's out of pure hunger and determination to embrace the beauty that our eyes are beholding.

1 tablespoon extra-virgin olive oil

1 red bell pepper (red capsicum), cut into strips

1 yellow onion, thinly sliced

2 garlic cloves, finely chopped

1 teaspoon finely chopped fresh red chile

Sprig of fresh thyme, leaves picked

14 ounces (400 g) sourdough pizza dough (ask your local bakery for some of their starter if you don't have any) or my New York Pizza dough (see page 32)

4 slices of double cream Brie

Sea salt and freshly ground black pepper

Heat the olive oil in a cast-iron frying pan with a lid or a Dutch oven over low heat (please note it needs to be cast-iron; otherwise the pizza dough won't cook properly). Add the red bell pepper strips, onion, garlic, chopped fresh chile and thyme and cook, stirring occasionally, for 3 minutes or until the onion is translucent.

Transfer the onion mixture to a bowl and wipe the pan or Dutch oven clean with a paper towel. Set over high heat, cover with the lid, and heat until it's HOT!

Using your hands, shape the dough into a circle that's roughly the same size as your pan. Very carefully transfer the dough to the hot pan and scatter over the onion mixture. Top with the brie and season with salt and pepper, then cover with the hot lid, reduce the heat to low, and cook for about 8 minutes. Remove the lid and carefully lift one side of the pizza to check that the base is lightly golden and the side is puffed up. The top should bounce back when lightly touched.

Allow the pizza to rest in the pan for 5 minutes, then carefully lift it out, cut into slices and serve.

Barbacoa

Put simply, barbacoa is an ancient style of barbecue that dates back to the Aztecs. Traditionally, a deep hole was dug into the earth, and the base lined with very hot coals and agave leaves. Meat, such as small game meats, birds and sometimes fish, were added and then covered with more agave leaves to trap in moisture. The hole was then covered with earth and the meat left to slow-cook–almost steam — all day or overnight.

I've used Cape Grim Tasmanian beef here, but feel free to change up the protein to use any game meat you've hunted. You could also try cooking it in the ground for a truly authentic experience. I made my barbacoa before heading on my adventure, it keeps really well and makes for a great breakfast taco post-surf.

1 (3-pound/1.35 kg) rump cap

2 tablespoons vegetable oil

Sea salt and freshly ground black pepper

1¼ cups (310 ml) beef broth, divided

3 to 4 chipotle chiles in adobo sauce (from 1 can), finely chopped

6 garlic cloves, finely chopped

1½ tablespoons ground cumin

1 tablespoon dried oregano

¼ teaspoon ground cloves

3 bay leaves

¼ cup (60 ml) freshly squeezed lime juice

Warm corn tortillas, to serve

Toppings of your choice, to serve

Light a fire and let it burn down for 1 hour until you obtain a medium heat. Set a grill grate over the fire.

Cut the rump cap into six portions and remove any large pieces of fat. Heat 1 tablespoon of the vegetable oil in a large cast-iron frying pan or Dutch oven. Pat the roast dry with paper towels and season with salt and pepper. Add three pieces to the pan and sear until browned on all sides. Repeat with the remaining oil and meat, then nestle the beef portions side by side in an even layer in the Dutch oven.

Combine the beef broth, chipotle, garlic, cumin, oregano and cloves in a small bowl, then pour the mixture over the meat. Nestle the bay leaves in among the beef, then cover and cook in the coals for about 5 hours.

Carefully remove the beef from the pot and use two forks to shred the meat. Stir the lime juice into the broth, then add the shredded beef and cook for a final 20 to 30 minutes over low heat. Strain the liquid from the beef and serve in warm tortillas with your favorite taco toppings.

Feeds 6

Equipment: Charcoal or gas
barbecue grill• Grill grate
• Cast-iron Dutch oven

Beef with Red Wine Onions

When I was writing my first cookbook, I took a road trip across the United States, where I had the pleasure of cooking with my good friend Kevin O'Conner. We cooked this dish for locals at an olive grove — I had brought along with me on the journey an abundance of steak given to me by my Tasmanian farming friends from Cape Grim Tasmania. Okay, I know you're thinking, You're in the USA, girl, eat our meat! But to be fair, it's nice to have a little piece of home with you wherever you go. Of course you can buy delicious beef here in the States; just make sure you seek out sustainably produced meat, and try to know your farmer where you can.

2 red onions, sliced into rings

A few fresh thyme sprigs

2 cups (500 ml) dry red wine

4 (9-ounce/250 g) Strip loin steaks

Sea salt

Heat your cooker (I used my Cadac portable grill with a grill plate attachment), the grill should be sizzling hot.

Place the onion rings in a Dutch oven and arrange the thyme sprigs around the side. Pour the wine over the top, then cover with the lid and place over low heat (an area of the grill without many coals; use tongs to move a few coals if necessary). Simmer gently for 20 to 30 minutes or until the onion is soft and translucent and the red wine has reduced to a runny sauce.

Add the steak to the hot part of the grill, sprinkle with salt and cook until the meat is medium-rare — depending on the thickness of the steaks, this should take about 5 minutes — with an internal temperature of 130°F (54°C). Allow the steaks to rest, covered, for 5 to 10 minutes before slicing — the internal temperature will increase a little to yield a perfectly cooked medium-rare steak.

Slice the steaks and serve with the onions and red wine sauce.

<u>Main</u>   Feeds 4   Equipment: Gas cooker or charcoal
                                                        barbecue • Cast-iron • Dutch oven

Peppercorn Fish

California has such a great variety of fish and a surprising abundance of pink peppercorn trees. Pink peppercorn leaves have a lot of oils in them and make for a great stuffing for fish, infusing it with flavor while it cooks. I had the pleasure of cooking with my dear friends Matt and Emma, who owned a very cool hotel in Malibu called The Surfrider. We made this fish and enjoyed Margaritas on a beautiful Southern California evening.

3 small whole white fish (about 14 oz/400 g each), such as snapper, gutted, skin on, scales removed

6 handfuls of pink peppercorn leaves, wild fennel or fresh flat-leaf parsley leaves

Salt

Extra-virgin olive oil, for drizzling

Lemon wedges, to serve

Light your fire and let it burn down for 1 hour until you obtain a medium heat.

Stuff your fish with the pink peppercorn leaves, then tie string around the fish so it stays intact. Tie some more string around the tail of the fish.

Hang the fish over the fire about 12 inches (30 cm) from the flame or coals. Cook for 45 minutes or until the eyes of the fish go white.

Season with salt, drizzle with olive oil and serve with lemon wedges for squeezing over.

Feeds 6

Equipment: Tripod • String
or garden wire

Ceviche with Leche de Tigre

Ceviche is enjoyed throughout Central and South America, where it's made with locally caught fish and shellfish. My dear South American friend Juan introduced me to this Peruvian version, and it's been a staple at most of the events we have done together over the years. Leche de Tigre ("tiger's milk") is the citrus-based marinade that "cooks" or cures the fish and it's what makes this ceviche so refreshing. But the addition of coconut cream makes it really special. Be sure you have a spoon handy for the sauce.

10 ounces (300 g) mahi mahi fillets (or other sashimi-grade fish), skin and bones removed

1 cup (250 ml) fish stock, chilled

1 cup (250 ml) coconut cream (from 13.5-ounce/400 ml can), chilled

1 mango, flesh cut into cubes

1 bird's eye chile, deseeded and finely chopped

8 tarragon leaves, finely chopped

8 flat-leaf parsley leaves, finely chopped

Finely grated zest and juice of 1 lime

1 red onion, thinly sliced

Tortilla chips, to serve (optional)

Cut the mahi mahi into ½-inch (1 cm) cubes and place in a glass or ceramic bowl.

To make the leche de tigre, combine ½ cup (85 g) of the cubed fish with the fish stock in a blender and process until blended.

Pour the blended fish mixture over the fish in the bowl and add the remaining ingredients. Mix well with your hands until completely combined. Serve immediately, fresh and delicious, with tortilla chips on the side for scooping up the ceviche, if you like.

Note: Instead of the mango you can also try ½ cup (83 g) blackberries and ½ cup (83 g) of stone fruit such as plum or peach.

<u>Main</u>   Feeds 4   Equipment: Blender

Planked Salmon with Lemon Yogurt

Native American tribes of the Pacific Northwest revere salmon, and many define themselves as Salmon People; it is a sacred food. There are five varieties of wild American salmon in the region: king salmon (Chinook), sockeye (red) salmon, coho (silver) salmon, pink (humpback) salmon, and chum (dog) salmon, with chinook, sockeye, and coho being the most well-known. Adding wild fennel fronds to the dry rub perfumes the fish with a note of light anise flavor. You can forage for wild fennel if it grows in your area, or even grow it from seed. Fresh dill is a good substitute if you don't have access to wild fennel.

1½ pounds (680 g) side of salmon, skin on

Sea salt and freshly ground black pepper

Handful of wild fennel fronds and flowers (or substitute with fresh dill or other herbs that complement the salmon)

Handful of wild fennel seeds and fronds, finely diced

2 tablespoons brown sugar

2 tablespoons sea salt

Zest of 1 lemon

Extra-virgin olive oil

1 tablespoon freshly squeezed lemon juice

Lemon Yogurt

1 cup (260 g) yogurt

Zest of 1 lemon

1 tablespoon small dill sprigs, plus extra to serve

1 tablespoon capers, rinsed, plus extra to serve

Pinch of sea salt

Soak the cedar plank in salted water for 2 hours, then drain. After 1½ hours, light your fire and let it burn for 30 minutes — you want a radiant heat to cook the salmon.

The Roccbox needs to be fully saturated with heat with the flame turned to low — you may need to turn it up slightly in between fillets to ensure the stone floor is at the desired temperature (about 350°F/180°C on the dial and 400–420°F/200–210°C on the stone floor).

Slice the salmon fillet crossways about 1 inch (2.5 cm) apart, but be careful not to go all the way through to the skin. This will help it cook easily and also make it easy to portion. Remove the bones from the salmon fillet and generously season the salmon with salt and pepper on both sides.

Lay the salmon, skin-side down on the cedar plank. To make the seasoning rub, in a bowl, add the wild fennel seeds and diced fronds, brown sugar, salt, and lemon, and mix until combined. Drizzle some olive oil over the salmon, using your hands to smear it over the fish, then sprinkle the seasoning rub over the top and sides of the fish.

>>

Main   Feeds 4   Equipment: 6 x 14 inch (15 x 35 cm) cedar plank • Gozney Roccbox portable pizza oven

Place in the Roccbox, and cook for 10 to 15 minutess, I like mine
a little underdone.

To make the lemon yogurt, place the yogurt, lemon zest,
dill, capers and salt in a bowl and mix to combine.

To serve, top the smoked salmon with the lemon yogurt.

Note: This dish is also excellent with a fried egg, sunny-side up.

Barbecued Peach & Prosciutto Salad with Fennel

Turns out peaches are not just a Southern thing in the US — they grow incredible peaches all along the West Coast. I've been so impressed with the produce in California. This recipe is simple and relies on the quality of its few ingredients. It's seasonal to summer, but definitely worth the wait.

6 peaches, halved, stones removed

1 fennel bulb, thinly sliced

10 slices (or more!) good-quality prosciutto

3 endives sliced lengthways, and leaves removed

Sea salt

Extra-virgin olive oil, for drizzling

Lemon wedges, to serve

Light a fire and let it burn down for about an hour until you obtain a medium heat. Place a grill grate over the fire.

Place the peach halves, cut-side down, on the grill and cook for about 10 minutes or until softened and slightly charred. Remove from the grill and slice the peach halves into quarters. Place the prosciutto on the grill and allow to get a little crispy. Remove.

Arrange the fennel, endive leaves and grilled peaches on a serving plate and drape the prosciutto over the top. Season with salt and finish with a good drizzle of olive oil. Serve with lemon wedges for squeezing over.

Side   Feeds 4   Equipment: Grill grate

Tomato & Crouton Salad

Tomatoes come thick and fast in California — when the season is on, it's *on*. You must eat them. This salad is quick and easy and goes with most proteins. It's a great one to remember and I love the addition of croutons. I find the crunch perfect with the sweet, juicy tomatoes.

3 tablespoons olive oil, plus ¼ cup (60 ml)

3 cloves garlic, minced

Salt and freshly ground black pepper

½ loaf fresh crusty bread, cut into small cubes

3 tablespoons red wine vinegar

2 pints (500 g) mixed tomatoes, such as heirloom and Roma, halved

8 ounces (280 g) bocconcini

8 basil leaves, chopped, plus extra for garnish

In a small skillet over medium-low heat, add 3 tablespoons olive oil, the butter, garlic, red pepper flakes, and salt and pepper, to taste. Cook to infuse the oil with the garlic, about 4 minutes.

Add the cubed bread to a large bowl, pour the garlic mixture over the bread and toss to coat. Place in a frying pan over the heat and allow to get golden brown and crunchy; this should take about 5 minutes.

In a small bowl, whisk together the remaining olive oil and red wine vinegar with chopped basil and set aside.

In a large serving bowl, combine the tomatoes, mozzarella, croutons, basil, and the oil and vinegar mixture. Gently toss to coat all the tomatoes and croutons.

If you happen across some wild fennel, toss some through the salad for a bit of extra wild flavor.

Side   Feeds 4   Equipment: Gas cooker • Large saucepan • Frying pan

Coconut Cookies

Dehydrating cookies is the way to go if you're heading out on a long hike. You can, of course, bake them in the oven, but using a dehydrator ensures that they last a lot longer and you're guaranteed something yummy on the trail.

2 large eggs

4 tablespoons superfine (caster) sugar

2 cups (190 g) unsweetened coconut flakes

Pinch of sea salt

½ cup (95 g) chopped semisweet chocolate or semisweet chocolate chips

⅓ cup (75 g) salted butter, melted and cooled to room temperature

Flaked sea salt, to serve

Preheat a dehydrator to 130°F (54°C). Line a tray with parchment paper.

In a bowl, whisk the eggs and sugar until light and fluffy. Add the coconut flakes, sea salt, chocolate and butter and stir until combined.

Let the batter sit for 20 minutes so that the coconut can absorb some of the liquid and swell.

Spoon piles of the cookie mixture onto the prepared tray and shape into round discs (best for packing in your backpack) — you should get about 15 cookies. Sprinkle the cookies with flaked sea salt, then transfer to the dehydrator and dehydrate for 9 hours.

Once dehydrated, the cookies will keep for up to 1 month. Enjoy!

Sweets   Feeds 8   Equipment: Dehydrator

MAGIC IN
THE DESERT

A CULINARY OASIS FROM JOSHUA TREE & TEXAS TO BAJA

Before starting out on this Wild American Road Trip, I had so many preconceived ideas around the landscape and what to expect from each destination. In the very simplest of ways I conjured images of Joshua Tree and barren desert, Texas and BBQs, and when I thought of Mexico, I pictured bright, sunny palm trees. Of course, those elements are all there, but this wild landscape is a far greater feast for the eyes (and all the senses, really) than I ever imagined it to be.

Having undergone a sensory awakening to all the tastes and smells in front of me on this leg of the trip, it stirred a desire to learn more about the indigenous history here, specifically around food. I wanted to understand, and taste, smell and see what America's First Peoples had eaten in this very place, so many years before me. And as I researched Texas, for example, and dug a little deeper, I found it was steeped in Native American history, a culture rich in wild food and foraged ingredients.

Take the "Magic Eight" plants, for example. Think: corn, beans, squash, chiles, tomatoes, potatoes, vanilla, and cacao. These are eight plants that Native peoples gave to the world and are now woven into almost every cuisine. But we can break that Magic Eight down even further, with, for example, the "Three Sisters," which refers to corn, beans and squash, plants that form the bedrock of the Indigenous American diet. Besides tasting incredible and having a high nutritional value, they're considered the trifecta of agricultural sustainability because of how well they grow together. Have a closer look at those ingredients. Not only are they indigenous foods in America, but they're also staples in Mexican food.

With Mexico and Texas sharing a border, the food influence between the two regions is undeniable and it made me consider that we may need to think about food as being part of a landscape, rather than it having a nationality, which makes sense really, given that food comes from nature. It's neat when you think about it.

Indigenous people transformed the landscape's plants and animals into food across all seasons. They hunted pronghorn, deer, rabbits, turkeys, and quail; harvested persimmons, mustang grapes, and pecans; and ground acorns and mesquite pods into flour. Game meat was highly sought after, and when you consider a Texan's love of a BBQ today, it's not hard to join the dots to a history that predates us all.

At some point, there was a fusion between this region's traditional food and the new world (thanks to European imports). For example, today's Mexican food found in the US is often laden with additions. However, cooking traditionally, reminded me that traditional Mexican food — much like albóndigas (meatballs usually served with a broth or sauce) — is actually very clean, colorful and fresh in flavor. And that's also in part because of how this food is prepared. You might be used to thinking that Mexican dishes are quick to prepare, but with these recipes, it's important to take your time. Whether it's in the way you cook your

meat in the ground over coals, or how you assemble the food on your plate, a deeper consideration around how you produce your meal, will ensure you're making delicious, authentic food, just the way it was designed to be made.

I'm learning on this journey with you, so as we embark on our travels throughout Texas, Joshua Tree and Baja, it's a little less about cowboy hats and boots this time around (although, I do love those), and it's more about discovering the roots of the foods we utilize, and understanding how we can make food taste great, together.

Machaca con Huevos

This is an easy, savory breakfast from the northern states of Mexico made with eggs and the famous machaca (shredded dry beef). Traditionally, strips of beef were dried under the searing heat of the sun, which preserved the meat, but today more modern techniques are used. The dried beef is then pounded before being added to dishes, or rehydrated in broths. You can make machaca at home if you have a dehydrator (see page 140) or simply use store-bought machaca de res (beef) in this dish.

5 large eggs

Sea salt and freshly ground black pepper

2 tablespoons vegetable or canola oil

1 cup (130 g) diced onion (red, yellow or white are all fine)

1 Anaheim pepper, diced

2 large tomatoes, chopped

2 cups (400 g) chopped machaca (see page 140)

To serve

Warm corn tortillas

Crumbled queso fresco

Cooked beans of your choice

In a small bowl, whisk the eggs and season to taste with salt and pepper. Set aside.

Light a fire and let it burn down for about an hour until you obtain a medium heat. Place a grill grate over the fire. Heat the oil in a large cast-iron frying pan over medium heat. Add the onions and Anaheim pepper, and cook for 3 minutes or until soft. Add the tomatoes and cook for 2 minutes, then add the machaca and stir to combine. Set aside.

Heat a separate cast-iron frying pan over low heat, add the beaten egg and use a spatula to fold the egg until it's just scrambled and cooked through, about 2 to 4 minutes. Take care not to overcook the egg — you want to pull it off the heat just as it comes together, as the residual heat will continue to cook the egg.

Serve the scrambled eggs warm with the machaca tomatoes, warm tortillas, crumbled queso fresco and your favorite beans.

Feeds 4

Equipment: Grill grate • Cast-iron
frying pan

Machaca

The great thing about this recipe is that you can use this in many dishes or eat as a form of jerky. For example, you can take it with you on a hike as a snack or you can chop it into bits and rehydrate to use in a dish. I used the rump cap from Cape Grim beef in Tasmania — I'm always sentimental when I travel, so it's nice to be able to bring a little of my home with me and share it with others around the campfire or hiking trail.

2 pounds (900 g) trimmed rump cap, excess fat removed

2 teaspoons freshly ground black pepper

1½ tablespoons fine sea salt

Using a sharp knife, slice the rump cap against the grain into 1-inch (2.5 cm) pieces, about ⅛ inch (5 mm) thick. In a large bowl, toss the beef strips with the black pepper, and salt until evenly coated.

Arrange the beef on wire racks in a single layer, making sure none of the pieces are touching. Place both wire racks in the dehydrator and dehydrate for 6 hours. Remove from the dehydrator and let the machaca cool completely.

Working with a few slices of machaca at a time, cut the pieces into ¼-inch (5 mm) strips. Transfer to a mortar and pestle and pound until you have light, fluffy bits of beef that resemble cotton candy — bizarre but delicious. Repeat with the remaining machaca.

To store, keep the machaca in an airtight container. It will keep for up to 6 months.

Breakfast & Brunch   Makes 1 pound (500g)   Equipment: Dehydrator • Mortar

Bacon Tater Tots

Tater tots are little pillows of golden bliss. I always think, why have a French fry when you have clouds of potato? I believe these tater tots could be the next big thing in the culinary world. I also think they are fantastic eaten for breakfast. Maybe you think I'm mad, but I'm just potato obsessed! If you don't have a pizza oven, you can make these on the stovetop, too.

10½ ounces (300 g) Russet or other floury potatoes

1½ ounces (45 g) duck fat

Sea salt and freshly ground black pepper

6 slices bacon (streaky bacon), thinly sliced

Preheat your your Gozney Roccbox portable pizza oven to 480°F (250°C).

Peel and grate the potatoes and squeeze out all the liquid, then transfer to a large bowl.

Melt the duck fat in a frying pan, then mix three-quarters of the melted fat through the grated potato, along with some salt and pepper. Cook the bacon in the same frying pan, then set aside to cool. Mix the bacon through the potato.

Add the remaining duck fat to the pan and heat the pan in the pizza oven at 480°F (250°C) until it's super hot.

Using your fingers, mold the potato mixture into small 1-inch (2.5 cm) cubes, then carefully place the tater tots in the hot pan. Cook, rotating as needed, for 2 to 4 minutes until cooked through, crispy and golden brown.

Serve the tater tots on their own or with eggs on toast for breakfast.

Breakfast & Brunch

Feeds 2

Equipment: Gozney Roccbox
portable pizza oven • Box grater

Leftover Beef Breakfast

I was screaming along Interstate 10, from Florida to California, where I was relocating. It was around 8 o'clock in the morning, and my friend suggested we stop off in Louisiana for a bite to eat — she assured me it was worth the 30 minute detour. We whipped off the highway with my Defender trailer in tow that was loaded to exploding with my life. I nervously drove down some brightly colored streets and was relieved when I saw an easy car park to pull into. As we sat down in the nearest restaurant, I noticed an unusual amount of beef on the menu for breakfast. Although not accustomed to such a heavy morning meal, it seemed an obvious choice to try the locals' favorite, and I wasn't disappointed. It was so good that I felt it deserved a place in this book. This breakfast is perfect if you are heading out for a big day hiking or other such adventures, as it will fill you up for hours. You can use whatever cut of beef you like — I enjoyed some Wanderer flank steak from Australia with my breakfast.

8 ounces (220 g) flank steak or rump cap, cooked to your liking

Coarse sea salt

1 pound (450 g) sweet potatoes, peeled and cut into ³⁄₄-inch (2 cm) chunks

1 pound (450 g) red-skinned potatoes, unpeeled, cut into ³⁄₄-inch (2 cm) chunks

½ cup (130 g) sour cream

1 tablespoon finely grated fresh horseradish or prepared horseradish

2 teaspoons freshly squeezed lemon juice

¼ cup (60 ml) extra-virgin olive oil, divided, plus extra for brushing

1 small red onion, thinly sliced

Freshly ground black pepper

4 eggs, fried

¼ cup (15 g) chopped mixed herbs, such as dill, parsley, chives, tarragon

>>

Breakfast & Brunch
         Feeds 4
         Equipment: Grill grate or charcoal barbecue • Cast-iron frying pan

147

Light your fire and let it burn down for 1 hour until you obtain a medium heat. Set a grill grate 12 inches (30 cm) over the coals.

Cut the beef into steaks 1-inch (2.5 cm) thick, following the grain of the meat. Season the steaks with sea salt. To cook the steaks, place them on the grill grate.

Grill steaks directly over the coals, searing and turning once, until the internal temperature reaches 130°F (55°C) and a nice crust has developed.

Take the steaks off the heat and rest for 5 to 10 minutes before slicing.

Place the sweet potato and red-skinned potato in a pot and add enough water to cover the potato by 1 inch (2.5 cm). Season with a few big pinches of salt and bring to the boil over high heat. Lower the heat to maintain a gentle simmer and cook the potato for 5 to 8 minutes, until tender when pierced with a fork. Drain well and spread the potato on a clean kitchen towel to dry.

In a small bowl, mix the sour cream, horseradish, lemon juice, and ½ teaspoon of salt. Taste and adjust the seasoning if necessary, then set aside.

Heat 2 tablespoons of the olive oil in a large cast-iron skillet over medium–high heat until it just begins to smoke. Add the onion and cook, stirring frequently, for 5 to 6 minutes, until tender and nicely browned with a few charred edges. Season with salt, then transfer to a small bowl.

Heat the remaining 2 tablespoons of oil in the same skillet over high heat. When it just begins to smoke, add the potato and toss to coat it in the oil, then spread out in a single layer. Let the potato cook on one side, without moving, for 5 minutes, to develop a crust.

Stir the potato, scraping any sticky bits on the base of the pan, and cook for another 2 minutes.

Add the beef and continue cooking, occasionally turning the mixture gently, for 2 to 3 minutes, until the potato is evenly browned and crusty and the meat is heated through. Return the onion to the pan, season with pepper, and continue cooking for about 1 minute. Remove the pan from the heat, taste, and adjust the seasoning if necessary.

Top the beef and potato mixture with big dollops of the horseradish cream, place the fried eggs on top of the sauce, garnish with the herbs and a little more pepper, and serve.

Fire Fish Tacos

A day spent surfing off the Baja coast often ends with a few of us going spearfishing. At least for my friend Hanna, that is the case. She always rocks up to camp with some fresh fish and a big smile. Thanks, Hanna! It's a fun activity and a great way to source dinner while the fire heats up. I love this recipe as it's so easy to put together, and requires few, if any, utensils. You can premix your spices and bring them in a container to make this dish even easier.

4 skin-on white fish fillets, such as mahi mahi, snapper, sea bass or black cod

Warm corn tortillas, to serve

Salsa of your choice, to serve

Lemon wedges, to serve

Rub

1 tablespoon freshly ground black pepper

2¼ teaspoons dried thyme

2¼ teaspoons dried oregano

1½ teaspoons sweet paprika

1½ teaspoons garlic powder

1½ teaspoons sea salt

1 teaspoon ground white pepper

1 teaspoon cayenne pepper

1 tablespoon extra-virgin olive oil, plus extra for grilling

Light the fire and let it burn down for about 1 hour until you obtain a medium heat. Place a grill grate about 8 inches (20 cm) above the coals.

In a small bowl, whisk together the black pepper, thyme, oregano, paprika, garlic powder, sea salt, white pepper, and cayenne pepper. Add the extra-virgin olive oil and stir to combine.

Pat the fish fillets dry with paper towels, then coat both sides of each fillet with the rub until completely coated. Set the fish aside at room temperature for 15 minutes for the flavors to infuse.

To cook the fish, coat both sides of the fillets with olive oil and place skin-side down on the grill, and cook each side for 5 to 8 minutes, until opaque with crispy skin.

To serve, divide the fish among tortillas, spoon over some salsa and squeeze with lemon juice.

Main   Feeds 6   Equipment: Grill grate

Caldo de Albóndigas

Although albóndigas are a popular Mexican food, they actually originated in Spain during the period of Muslim rule (AD 711 to 1031). The word itself derives from the Arabic *al-bunduq* which translates to "hazelnut" and describes things that are small and round, such as these little meatballs. Albóndigas then traveled to Mexico from Spain with the conquistadors. The ingredients used to make albóndigas were highly influenced by the different places the recipe traveled to throughout the years, adding to its uniqueness. When served like this in a simmering, spicy broth with tender veggies, they make for a warm and nourishing meal. Maybe that's why some call this dish "Mexican soul food."

4 carrots, sliced

2 small potatoes, peeled and diced

1 medium onion, diced

1 ½ cups (375 ml) salsa (medium or hot)

2 beef bouillon cubes

1½ pounds (680 g) ground (minced) beef

⅓ cup (30 g) seasoned dry breadcrumbs

⅓ cup (80 ml) milk

1 tablespoon chopped fresh cilantro (coriander)

Bring 4 cups (1 L) of water, the carrots, potatoes, onion, salsa, and bouillon cubes to the boil in a large saucepan. Reduce the heat to a medium simmer and cook, stirring occasionally, for 10 minutes.

Meanwhile, mix together the beef, breadcrumbs, and milk in a bowl. Form the mixture into 1-inch (2.5 cm) meatballs and drop them into the simmering broth. Return the broth to the boil, then reduce the heat to medium–low. Cover and cook until the meatballs are no longer pink in the center and the vegetables are tender, about 20 minutes. Sprinkle with the cilantro and serve.

Main   Feeds 4

Confit Antelope Ribs

You can confit the ribs outdoors or at home in the oven before you set off on your adventure. If you confit the ribs at home ahead of time, this is an easy recipe to have in your cooler ready to grill. I have used antelope here, as it's a readily available wild animal in the area. It's also a delicious way to try other proteins that have less of an environmental footprint.

3½ pounds (1.5 kg) antelope ribs

3 tablespoons salt

Olive oil, as needed for cooking the ribs

1 tablespoon fennel seeds

1 tablespoon cumin seeds

¼ cup plus 3 tablespoons (100 ml) molasses

3 tablespoons balsamic vinegar

3 tablespoons red wine

Sprinkle the ribs all over with the salt. Arrange them on a tray and chill for 8 hours or overnight.

Light your fire and let it burn down for 1 hour until you obtain a medium heat. Place a grill grate about 12 inches (30 cm) above the coals.

Rinse the ribs, pat dry, and put in a Dutch oven, drenching them in olive oil. Heat on the grill until the olive oil starts to bubble.

Place the lid on the Dutch oven, then place in the coals of the fire for approximately 2 hours, or until the ribs are tender and the meat comes easily away from the bone. Take the ribs out of the oil and chill until firm.

Combine the spices in a cast-iron frying pan over a low heat and toast until fragrant, then add the molasses, balsamic vinegar and red wine. Continue to cook the syrup until it reduces a little, by about one-third.

When the ribs are firm, place on the grill and allow to get a little more color and warm through. Then toss through the syrup and serve.

<u>Main</u>

Feeds 6

Equipment: Breeo Fire Pit and Outpost Grill or grill grate • Cast-iron Dutch oven • Cast-iron frying pan

Prickly Pear Glazed Venison Skewers

I first made a dish using these ingredients for an event outside of Austin. I made a venison tartare with the prickly pear and foraged leaves including wood sorrel. Here, I've used the venison and prickly pear to make skewers.

1 cup (150 g) diced peeled prickly pear

¼ cup (60 ml) freshly squeezed lemon juice

1 teaspoon dried red chili flakes

½ cup (100 g) raw sugar

1 pound (450 g) venison backstrap

Sea salt

Place the prickly pear, lemon juice, chili flakes, sugar and ½ cup (125 ml) of water in a saucepan over medium heat. Simmer for about 1 hour, until you have a runny jam consistency. To check if the jam is ready, place a little jam on the back of a metal spoon and run your finger through the middle. If the jam doesn't fill the space left behind by your finger, it is ready. If not, cook for a little longer and test again. Set aside to cool.

Meanwhile, soak 8 to 10 skewers or foraged sticks in water for about 30 minutes. Heat a charcoal or gas grill until very hot.

Thinly slice the venison, then toss to coat in the cooled jam. Tightly thread the venison onto the prepared skewers or foraged sticks, so they resemble kebabs.

Place the skewers on the grill, season with salt, and cook, turning frequently, for about 6 minutes, until charred and sticky.

Serve immediately.

Main   Feeds 4   Equipment: Charcoal or gas
                                                   barbecue grill • Saucepan • 8-10
                                                   skewers or foraged sticks

Whole Bird with Wojapi Sauce

We don't get wild turkey in Australia, other than a bush turkey that you definitely wouldn't eat — it would be as tough as nails! When I came to the USA, I was so excited to hunt and cook a wild turkey, and I have since been educated about their important history with the Native American people, who utilized every part of the animal: the meat was used for food; their feathers were used as fletching on arrows, and in headdresses and clothing; and their bones were used for tools, including scratchers for ritual ceremonies. Heritage turkeys have a much richer flavor than the breeds that you can buy at supermarkets.

This is my interpretation of the dish, which I'm honored to be able to cook, thanks to the preservation of native animals. I have made this with chicken as turkey isn't available year round, but feel free to switch out your poultry. The recipe works great both ways.

1 whole chicken (about 5 pounds/2.3 kg)

Coarse sea salt

2 cups (330 g) raspberries or blackberries

½ cup (60 g) pistachios, lightly toasted and chopped

1 lemon

1 bunch thyme

3 cups (750 ml) chicken stock

2 medium leeks, cut into 3-inch (10 cm) pieces and rinsed

2 tablespoons extra-virgin olive oil

¼ cup (80 ml) maple syrup

Wojapi Sauce (see page 163), to serve

>>

Main   Feeds 6   Equipment: Tripod • Cast-iron
Dutch oven

Remove the giblets from the chicken cavity and discard or reserve for another use. Pat the chicken dry using paper towels. Rub the chicken all over with ½ teaspoon coarse salt per pound of chicken.

Combine the raspberries or blackberries and pistachios in a bowl. Stuff the mixture into the chicken cavity with this, add a whole lemon.

Place the chicken on a large baking sheet, breast-side up, then set aside in the fridge, uncovered, for 4 to 6 hours to dry out the skin (this will ensure a crispy skin as it roasts).

When you are ready to cook the chicken, allow it to come to room temperature.

Light your fire and let it burn down for 1 hour until you obtain a medium heat.

Pour the chicken stock into a Dutch oven large enough to fit the chicken and add the leeks. Place the chicken, breast-side up, on top of the leeks and tuck the wings underneath. Cover with the lid, place over the fire and roast for 30 minutes. Baste the chicken with the juices. Continue roasting the chicken, basting every 30 minutes, for 1 to 1½ hours, until an instant-read thermometer inserted into the thickest part of a thigh reaches 165°F (74°C).

Brush the maple syrup over the chicken, then transfer to a chopping board to rest for 30 minutes before carving.

Carve the chicken. Smear some berry sauce on each plate and serve with some of the stuffing.

Wojapi Sauce

2 cups (335 g) blueberries
 or chokecherries, fresh
 or frozen

½ cup (125 ml) maple syrup

Yields 2 cups (500 g)

In a saucepan over medium heat, simmer the berries and maple syrup, stirring occasionally, for 5 minutes, until the berries have broken down into a sauce.

Serve with the chicken on page 160.

Three Sisters

Native Americans referred to corn, bean, and squash as the "three sisters" because they thrive and nurture each other when planted together. After traveling the USA over the past 20 years, I often drove past fields of corn and squash. I think this is a beautiful recipe to make while traveling.

1 cup (200 g) dried hominy

1 cup (200 g) dried brown tepary beans

1 small butternut squash (about 1 pound/500 g), peeled, halved, seeds and membranes scraped away, flesh cut into 1-inch (2.5 cm) chunks

3 tablespoons olive oil

1 small onion, halved and thinly sliced

3 tablespoon Hatch chile powder or any mild smoked red chile powder

Sea salt

1 ½ cup chopped kale or spinach

1 cup feta cheese, crumbled

Place the hominy and tepary beans in separate bowls. Add enough water to each bowl to cover the ingredients, then set aside to soak overnight at room temperature.

The next day, light a fire and let it burn down for 1 hour until you obtain a medium heat.

Place a grill grate about 8 inches (20 cm) above the fire.

Drain the hominy and the beans and place them in separate large saucepans with tight-fitting lids. Add enough water to cover the hominy and tepary beans, then bring to the boil over the fire. Reduce the heat to a gentle simmer, then cover and cook, stirring occasionally for 2 hours, until tender. Reserve 2 cups (500 ml) of the cooking liquid, then drain the hominy and beans and set aside.

Toss the squash with 1 tablespoon of the oil and a pinch of salt. Arrange the squash in an even layer on the grill grate and roast, turning over halfway through cooking, for 20 minutes or until golden and very tender.

>>

Feeds 6

Equipment: Grill grate • 2 x Large
cast-iron frying pan • Skillet

In a large skillet, heat the remaining 2 tablespoons of oil over medium–high heat. Add the onion, chile powder, a generous pinch of salt and cook, stirring occasionally 8-10 minutes, until the onions are soft and golden in color. Add the reserved cooking liquid and bring to a simmer. Add the cooked hominy and beans to the skillet, then stir in the roasted squash and greens. Season to taste with salt and serve with some feta cheese.

Parmesan Potato "Pizza"

This recipe was an amazing fluke: I had some leftover potatoes from dinner the night before and decided to toss in some cheese. Little did I know it would create a new camp favorite recipe! You can make this as a starter, as a dinner side or even breakfast, when you add a fried egg or some bacon.

1 garlic bulb

3 tablespoons extra-virgin olive oil, plus extra for drizzling

1½ cups (330 g) mayonnaise

4 medium Russet potatoes, or other floury potatoes

2½ teaspoons whole black peppercorns, plus freshly ground black pepper

1½ cups (135 g) freshly grated Parmesan, divided

Flaky sea salt

To make the roasted garlic aioli, light your fire and let it burn down for 1 hour until you obtain a medium heat. Place a grill grate over the coals.

Trim the top of the garlic bulb so the cloves are exposed. Place the garlic on a square of aluminum foil, cut-side up, and drizzle with olive oil. Tightly wrap the garlic in the foil and roast on a grill grate or in the coals of the fire for 45 minutes or until the garlic is soft and caramelized. Set aside until cool enough to handle, then squeeze the cloves into a bowl and mash with a fork to form a paste. Add the mayonnaise and a little freshly ground black pepper, and mix until smooth. Chill the aioli until ready to use.

Scrub the potatoes, then thinly slice into ¼-inch-thick (5 mm) rounds. Place in a large pot of cold, salted water, then cover and bring to the boil over the fire. Remove the lid and gently boil the potato for 2½ to 5 minutes, until just fork-tender but still holding its shape.

While the potato is boiling, place the peppercorns in a small skillet over the heat. Toast, shaking the skillet occasionally, for about 5 minutes, until fragrant. Transfer the peppercorns to a mortar and finely crush into little pieces (but not a powder).

>>

Lightly drizzle a large cast-iron frying pan with olive oil. Evenly sprinkle with ½ cup (45 g) of the grated Parmesan, covering as much of the pan as possible.

Drain the potato, then blot the slices dry with paper towels, and transfer to a large bowl. Add the olive oil, some flaky sea salt, and most of the crushed peppercorns (reserving ¼ teaspoon for garnish). Using a silicone spatula, gently mix to combine.

Carefully place the potato on top of the Parmesan in an even layer making sure the slices are not overlapping. Sprinkle ½ cup (45 g) of the remaining Parmesan over the potato.

Place the frying pan over the fire and cook the potato for about 40 minutes, until the cheese is golden and the potato is crispy.

Remove from the fire then immediately transfer the cheesy potato to a serving tray. Top with the remaining Parmesan, reserved crushed peppercorns, and a little more flaky salt. Cut into slices and serve with the roasted garlic aioli for dipping.

Native American Baked Beans

I bet you didn't know this — baked beans is a Native American dish, originally made from beans indigenous to the Americas. English colonists adopted the dish from the Native peoples in the 17th century, which then spread through the United Stated and Canada and eventually found its way into cookbooks. Traditionally, Native Americans mixed beans, maple sugar, and bear fat in pots and placed them in "bean holes" in the ground. These were lined with hot rocks that slowly cooked the beans. I think it's time to return the credit for this humble dish to its rightful owners.

1 pound (450 g) black beans

3 pieces kombu

1 tablespoon olive oil

1 cup (125 g) sliced white onion

¼ cup (60 ml) molasses

2 teaspoons sea salt

3 teaspoons yellow mustard powder

2 tablespoons smoked paprika

1 teaspoon ground kelp

Freshly ground black pepper, to taste

Rinse the beans well in a colander, then place in a large bowl and add enough water to cover the beans. Add the kombu, then cover and set aside in the fridge overnight.

The next day, light a fire and let it burn down for 1 hour until you obtain a medium heat. Place a grill grate about 8 inches (20 cm) above the fire.

Drain the beans and kombu, then transfer to a large Dutch oven and add enough water to cover the beans. Bring to the boil in the coals of the fire, cover with a lid, and cook until tender for about 1 hour.

Meanwhile, heat the olive oil in a cast-iron frying pan over the fire, add the onion cook for 4 to 5 minutes, until softened.

Add the onion, molasses, salt, mustard powder, and paprika to the beans and stir to combine. Cover and leave the Dutch oven in the coals overnight. The next day, add the kelp, ground black pepper, to the beans and stir well. Taste and adjust the seasoning if necessary.

Allow the beans to cool until just warm — this will thicken the sauce and allow the flavors to amplify. Serve with eggs for breakfast or as a side dish.

Cheese & Tomato

Growing up being homeschooled has its advantages, one of them being able to raid the kitchen cupboard when you have a lunch break. A staple in our family was cheese on toast, perhaps with a slice of tomato every now and then. This is a great resource when on the road — it's easy, quick and flavor-filled. Especially at the tail end of summer with tomatoes in season.

2 cloves garlic, finely chopped

½ cup (125 ml) extra-virgin olive oil

Flour tortillas or thickly sliced sourdough bread

Cheese, such as cheddar or your favorite melting cheese (a melty cheese with a little salty flavor works best)

2 Roma tomatoes, sliced

Salt

Freshly ground black pepper

Hot sauce (optional)

Preheat your Gozney Roccbox to 400°F (205°C).

Once the pizza oven gets hot enough, you can start assembling your... "pizzas." (You can also do this on a grill or in a cast iron frying pan, but the pizza oven will get you evenly melted cheese and a golden color.)

Combine the garlic and the olive oil in a bowl. Brush the tortillas with the garlic oil, add cheese and tomatoes and season with salt and pepper. Using the pizza oven spatula, launch the tortillas one at a time into the oven and cook until the cheese is melted.

Serve with hot sauce if desired.

Feeds 3

Equipment: Gozney Roccbox
portable pizza oven

Churros with Chocolate Dipping Sauce

Crunchy on the outside, tender and airy on the inside, these deep-fried pastries dusted with cinnamon sugar are popular in Mexico and Spain. Yes, there are easier desserts that you can make on the road, but they are just so delicious and this recipe is easily adaptable for the campground. Although not traditional star-shaped churros (you're not going to whip out your piping bag while traveling), you can have some fun with the shapes you can make with a spoon. I guarantee you will make new friends as the smell of cinnamon wafts through the campsite!

6 tablespoons (90 g) unsalted butter

½ teaspoon sea salt

1 tablespoon granulated sugar

1 cup (120 g) all-purpose (plain) flour

4 eggs

1 teaspoon vanilla extract

Vegetable oil, for deep-frying

Cinnamon sugar

¾ cup (180 g) superfine (caster) sugar

2 teaspoons ground cinnamon

Chocolate dipping sauce

⅔ cup (140 g) chocolate chips

⅔ cup (160 ml) heavy whipping (double) cream

2 teaspoons ground cinnamon

Mix together the sugar and cinnamon in a shallow bowl and set aside. Light a fire and let it burn down for 1 hour until you obtain a medium heat. Place a grill grate about 12 inches (30 cm) above the fire.

In a large saucepan, bring 1 cup (250 ml) of water, the butter, salt and sugar to a rolling boil over medium–high heat. As soon as the mixture comes to the boil, immediately remove the pan from the heat.

Tip the flour into the pan and use a wooden spoon to stir vigorously for 30 to 60 seconds, until the flour is incorporated. Return the mixture to the heat and cook, stirring, for 30 seconds. Remove from the heat, add three of the eggs, one at a time, and beat, stopping to scrape down the bowl after each addition, until combined. Add the vanilla and mix until the dough is smooth and glossy, and the eggs are completely incorporated — the dough should be thick.

Set a tripod above the fire and heat enough oil for deep-frying in a large saucepan to 370°F (190°C). Working in batches of no more than three churros, add a dessert spoon of dough into the hot oil and deep-fry both sides for 1½ to 2 minutes, until golden brown.

>>

Sweets

Feeds 6

Meanwhile, to make the chocolate dipping sauce, place the chocolate chips, cream, and cinnamon in a small pot and over the fire, but just to the side, as you don't want to burn the chocolate. Let the chocolate simmer slowly and steadily, you want a nice smooth sauce.

Drain the churros on paper towels for 30 seconds, then toss in the cinnamon sugar. Serve with the chocolate dipping sauce.

Best Gluten-free Brownies

It's easy to load up on junk food when you're on the road. It's just too tempting to buy snacks for convenience that aren't always healthy, but may seem exciting in the moment. These delicious, sugar-free brownies are my go-to for a feel-good sweet treat while traveling.

1 cup (270 g) almond butter

2 ounces (60 g) dark chocolate (85 to 90% cocoa solids), melted

¼ cup (50 g) erythritol (or raw sugar)

¼ cup (20 g) almond meal

1 teaspoon baking powder

2 large eggs, beaten

Light a fire and let it burn down for 1 hour or until you obtain a medium heat. Set a grill grate 12 inches (30 cm) above the coals and set a tripod above the grill. Line a lidded Dutch oven with enough parchment (baking) paper to overhang the side by 2 inches (5 cm).

In a large bowl, combine the almond butter, melted chocolate and erythritol. Stir in the almond meal and baking powder, then gently fold in the eggs until combined.

Transfer the mixture to the Dutch oven, cover with the lid, then hang the oven from the tripod and shovel some hot coals on top. Cook the brownie for 15 to 20 minutes, until the top is lightly cracked, but still with a little wobble. When you remove the brownie from the fire, it will be very soft. Leave the brownie to cool for 20 minutes before removing from the oven and cutting into pieces.

Cookies & Mellows

Homemade graham crackers are way more delicious and will impress your friends or someone special. I suggest making the crackers before hitting the road, and then cooking the s'more once you reach your destination.

Graham crackers

2 cups (240 g) whole-wheat (wholemeal) flour, plus extra for dusting (do not use stone-ground or all-purpose/plain flour)

1 teaspoon ground cinnamon

1 teaspoon baking soda (bicarbonate of soda)

½ teaspoon sea salt

¼ cup plus 3 tablespoons (100 g) salted butter, at room temperature

1 cup (200 g) packed light brown sugar

3 tablespoons whole (full-cream) milk

⅓ cup (80 ml) honey

2 teaspoons vanilla extract

For the s'mores

1 tablespoon (15 g) salted butter

1 cup (270 g) peanut butter

2 (3½-ounce/100 g) dark chocolate bars, broken into pieces

2 cups (90 g) marshmallows (or make your own — you'll find a recipe in my first cookbook, *Wild Adventure*)

>>

To make the graham crackers, in a bowl, whisk together the flour, cinnamon, baking soda and salt. Set aside.

In a stand mixer fitted with the paddle attachment, or using an electric hand mixer, cream the butter and sugar on low speed. Increase the speed to medium and beat for about 3 minutes, until light and fluffy. Reduce the speed to low, add the flour mixture, and beat for about 2 minutes, until incorporated and a soft dough forms. Beat in the milk, honey and vanilla extract — the dough should be sticky and soft.

Divide the dough into two discs, wrap separately in plastic wrap, and chill for at least 1 hour.

Place an oven rack on the middle shelf of your oven and preheat the oven to 350°F (180°C).

Generously flour your work surface or a piece of parchment paper and place one disc of dough in the center. Gently press the dough into a 5 x 6 inch (12.5 x 15 cm) rectangle, then sprinkle with flour, flip over, and dust again. Working from the center outwards, and adding more flour as needed, roll the dough into a 11 x 15 inch (28 x 38 cm) rectangle. Slide the dough onto a baking sheet and brush away the excess flour. Repeat with the remaining dough disk.

For grocery store lookalike crackers, score each sheet of dough into twelve 2¼ x 4¾ inch (5.5 x 12 cm) rectangles, and dot with a bamboo skewer.

Transfer one of the baking sheets to the oven and bake for 10 to 12 minutes, until the crackers are firm and darkened. Remove from the oven and immediately cut along the pre-scored lines with a knife. Repeat with the remaining sheet of dough. Allow the crackers to cool to room temperature on the baking sheets, then package up and head out!

To make a giant s'more, light your fire and let it burn down for 1 hour until you obtain a medium heat. Alternatively, you can cook the s'more in a preheated 350°F (180°C) oven.

Smear the butter around the base of a cast-iron frying pan. Top with a layer of crackers, the peanut butter, chocolate and, finally, the marshmallows.

Place your pan in the coals of the fire and cook until the giant s'more is melted and gooey. It will only take about 5 minutes for the magic to happen, so keep an eye on it. Eat with more crackers.

Note: Of course, you can also thread the marshmallows onto sticks if you want to make traditional s'mores. Roast over the fire until they're charred and gooey, then sandwich with some chocolate between two crackers.

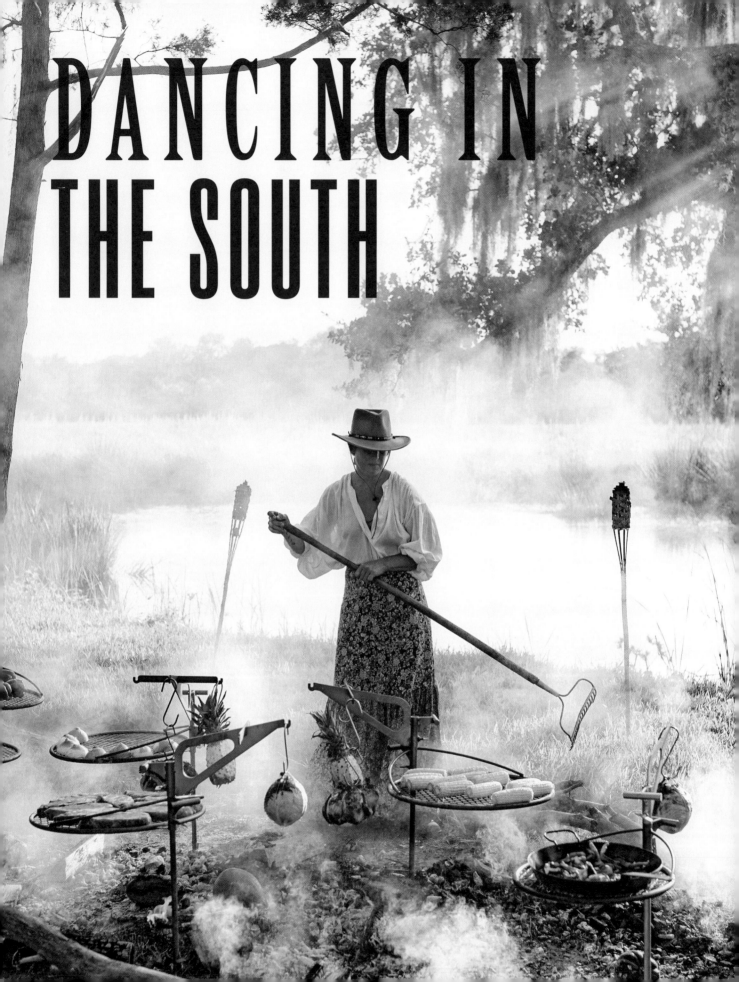

DANCING IN
THE SOUTH

TURN UP THE HEAT IN FLORIDA

Hello Florida, how good it feels to be back in your steamy (read: humid!) embrace. Over the years I've spent a fair amount of time living and exploring Florida, so parts of this state feel pretty personal. I met my first stateside mate, Vince, way back at a kid's summer camp in Virginia when I was sixteen. Vince lived on Amelia Island, just over an hour from St. Augustine, the nation's oldest city, and when I returned to the US at age twenty-four, my friend, his family and their friends showed me the region.

Among the delights of traveling to St. Augustine, Amelia Island, and Cumberland Island, Georgia, and exploring run-down clubs and jazz bars which have seen the likes of great vocalists such as Billie Holiday and Nina Simone once perform, what struck me so profoundly all that time ago, was the dark past of Florida: its history of the slave trade, and struggle for civil rights. As I listened and learned about the area's past, I recall being so taken aback by the

overarching concept of slavery, and by the unbelievable accounts around decades of regulations that restricted African Americans from living a life with basic human rights. It was unfathomable to me then, and it still is to me today.

And just as travel does, these early adventures in Florida opened the way to new emotions, new places, new experiences, new understanding, and in the process changed my perspective and expanded my ability for compassion and empathy. While St. Augustine was great, I vowed to my 24-year-old self that I probably wouldn't want to live there. Cut to twelve years later, and on a wing and a prayer I arrived back in Florida, where for the following nine months, St. Augustine would become my home as I transitioned to life back in the US of A. At this point, Florida became quite poignant in my personal and professional journey. It awakened a side of me that was lying dormant; it caught me, and gave me an outlet for my untapped creativity.

I'd removed myself from the comfort zone of my Australian network, and I was living among a great group of Floridians. Daunting as it was, I felt an affinity with my family in the Everglades state. Florida exposed me to a whole new way of life. Brimming with crabs, oysters, gators, and fish, it was here that I learned to hunt and fish in a whole new way. But it wasn't just the produce and cooking I grew to love, it was the lifestyle this area offered, which really spoke my language. Here, the beaches are thriving with families, trucks, outdoor grills and a sense of freedom that accompanies never-ending afternoons spent on big, long beaches that seemed to go forever.

Beach culture is alive, the friends I made here are lifers, and Florida in all its untamed, hurricane-prone glory, proved itself to be a soft place for me to land. To be back here again, in the steaming heat and familiar territory on my Wild American Road Trip, I feel comfortable, and yet conscious of the deep connection I have to this wild, brutal place. In a way, returning here, to my USA roots, was the perfect way to set off on this adventure.

Photos courtesy of THOR Industries.

Crawfish Boil

For hundreds of years, crawfishing has been a sustainable method of catching seafood throughout North America. From the Pacific Northwest to the Gulf Coast, across the Midwest, and along the Eastern Seaboard, Native Americans knew which treasures their lakes, rivers, swamps, and estuaries held.

When Cajun ancestors came to North America from France in the 1700s, they suffered many hardships, but slowly learned how to hunt and fish living alongside the local First Peoples in the area. By the 19th century, Cajun settlers in Louisiana adapted the lobster recipes they inherited from their ancestors on the Canadian coast by replacing the large crustaceans with crawfish. As a result, crawfishing became big business, and today 90-95 percent of the United States' commercial crawfish production comes from Louisiana.

I once ordered lobster in New England thinking it was crawfish, but it turned out it was not, and my bill was rather large as a result. (Crawfish are small and juicy; lobsters are large and sweet.)

Photo courtesy of THOR Industries.

1 tablespoon whole black peppercorns

1 tablespoon whole coriander seeds

2 tablespoons whole cloves

1½ tablespoons allspice berries

1 pound (450 g) sea salt

4 tablespoons cayenne pepper

2 tablespoons garlic powder

2 tablespoons smoked paprika

1 tablespoon onion powder

1 tablespoon dried thyme

1 tablespoon dried oregano

1 tablespoon mustard powder

1 tablespoon dried dill

6 dried bay leaves, crumbled

10 pounds (4.5 kg) live crawfish

3 pounds (1.3 kg) small red potatoes (halved if larger than 2 inches/5 cm in diameter)

8 ears of corn (sweetcorn), husks and silks removed, halved crosswise

2 garlic bulbs, unpeeled, cloves separated

1 pound (450 g) andouille sausage, cut into 1-inch (2.5 cm) pieces

>>

Main

Feeds a crowd

Equipment: Spice grinder • 40-quart
(39 L) crawfish pot with strainer
• Gas burner

Place the peppercorns, coriander seeds, cloves, and allspice berries in a spice grinder and grind for 10 to 15 seconds, until ground.

Fill a 40-quart (39 L) crawfish pot with the strainer inserted with 5 gallons (22 L) of water and add the freshly ground spices, salt, cayenne pepper, garlic powder, paprika, onion powder, thyme, oregano, mustard powder, dill, and bay leaves. Cover and bring to the boil over high heat — this will take about 40 minutes.

Meanwhile, rinse the crawfish thoroughly in the bag they came in to remove any excess dirt and mud. Put the crawfish in a large container and fill with cold water, then stir to remove any remaining dirt from the crawfish. Transfer small batches of crawfish to a colander and rinse under cool running water. Pick out any debris or dead crawfish. Once all the crawfish have been rinsed, discard the dirty water, and return the crawfish to the container. Repeat this process six to eight times, or until the water is clear.

When the seasoned water comes to the boil, add the potatoes, corn, garlic, and sausage. Cover and cook for 10 minutes, then add the crawfish and cook, covered, for 3 minutes. Ask a friend to help you and very carefully lift the larger strainer from the pot, leaving the water behind.

Serve the crawfish boil in the strainer on the table and gather your friends. Depending on how many friends you've invited, you may have to call in some extra people from the campsite to help you get through the huge quantities of seafood!

Beer-boiled Shrimp

I was off fishing for tarpon in Tampa, Florida, as the season had just started. The first day at sea resulted in no fish, so we drove the boat up to a cute little restaurant that was literally on the shore of the inlet (I love that there are restaurants where the tables are planted into the sand and the tide gently laps at your feet as you eat). On the menu were beer-boiled shrimp. I thought beer . . . BOILED? But also, YES! My fishing buddy Ryan assured me it was good, so we dove in with our bread. It didn't disappoint. One of my favorite things about Southern food is the joy of celebrating a freshly caught catch by eating your fill while standing or sitting with friends; no utensils, other than maybe a spoon. It's so primal, yet evokes such community.

1½ cups (12 ounces/350 ml) craft beer of your choice, such as wheat ale, Pilsner, pale ale or lager

1 onion, roughly chopped

3 lemon wedges, plus extra to serve

2 to 3 bay leaves

1 teaspoon mustard seeds

1 tablespoon Old Bay Seasoning

21 to 25 fresh shrimp (about 2 pounds/900 g), shelled and deveined

Large knob of butter

1 tablespoon finely chopped fresh parsley leaves

Bread, to serve (I like a French baguette sliced and toasted with garlic butter)

Light your fire and let it burn down for 1 hour until you obtain a medium heat. Pour the beer and 1½ cups (350 ml) of water into a large pot and bring to a simmer over medium–high heat. Add the onion, lemon wedges, bay leaves, mustard seeds and Old Bay Seasoning and simmer for 30 minutes. Add the shrimp and continue to simmer for 3 to 4 minutes, until the shrimp are just cooked through.

Using a slotted spoon, transfer the shrimp to a large bowl and add a good dollop of butter, along with the parsley leaves. Strain the broth and discard the aromatics.

Divide the shrimp among bowls and ladle the broth over the top.

Toast the bread with some garlic butter, if you like, and serve warm alongside the beer-boiled shrimp, dipping the bread into the broth.

Extra-Crispy Fried Chicken

I'm not sure I need to say too much about this recipe, other than it's ridiculously good. When you're in the South you need to deliver the best gosh-darn fried chicken recipe you can! Here's mine and I promise you it's worth the process. So gather your friends around and cook up some Southern-fried chicken. You will need to start this recipe 1 to 2 days ahead.

Photo courtesy of THOR Industries.

6 chicken breasts, bone in

6 chicken wings

3 chicken drumsticks

2 quarts (2 L) canola oil, for deep-frying

Hot sauce, to serve

Pickles, to serve

Buttermilk brine

6 cups (1.4 L) buttermilk

1 teaspoon sea salt

1 teaspoon smoked paprika

Dry mix

2 teaspoons sea salt

2 teaspoons smoked paprika

½ teaspoon ground white pepper

2 tablespoons garlic powder

2 cups (240 g) all-purpose (plain) flour

2 cups (280 g) rice flour

1 cup (100 g) tapioca flour

To make the buttermilk brine, combine the ingredients in a bowl and set aside.

Place the chicken in the buttermilk brine, making sure the pieces are submerged, and refrigerate overnight.

When you're ready to cook the chicken, combine the dry mix ingredients in a large bowl and set aside. Light your fire and let it burn down for 1 hour until you obtain a medium heat.

Double coat the chicken by dredging it thoroughly in the dry mix and making sure you really rub the mixture into the meat. Return the chicken to the buttermilk and then in the dry mix again — this will ensure a really crispy coating to sink your teeth into.

Heat the canola oil in a deep-fryer or large saucepan to 350°F (180°C). Working in batches, fry the chicken for about 15 minutes until crispy and golden and with an internal temperature of 165°F (75°C).

Drain the fried chicken on paper towels and serve with your favorite hot sauce and pickles.

<u>Main</u>   Feeds 4   Equipment: Charcoal or gas
                                                      barbecue grill• Large saucepan

Fried Green Tomato Burgers

I just love the name of these burgers! They are my take on the classic Southern way of preparing unripe (yep, that's why they're green) tomatoes. You can, of course, enjoy these fried green tomatoes on their own, but they're really fantastic in a bun smeared with my chipotle sauce. Heirloom green tomatoes are, in my opinion, the best.

Photo courtesy of THOR Industries.

Canola oil, for deep-frying

4 green (unripe) tomatoes, cut into ¼-inch-thick (5 mm) rounds

Flaked sea salt and freshly ground black pepper

Dry mix

2 teaspoons sea salt

2 teaspoons smoked paprika

½ teaspoon ground white pepper

2 tablespoons garlic powder

2 cups (240 g) all-purpose (plain) flour

2 cups (280 g) rice flour

1 cup (100 g) tapioca flour

4 eggs

2 tablespoons milk

Chipotle sauce

1 cup of good quality store bought mayonnaise

2 chipotle chilis from the can, diced finely

1 lime, juiced

Salt to taste

To serve (optional)

Burger buns of your choice, split

Butter lettuce leaves

Sliced long red chile, such as bird's eye (optional)

>>

Main   Feeds 4   Equipment: Charcoal or gas
barbecue grill • Saucepan

To make the chipotle sauce, combine the mayonnaise, chipotle chilis and lime juice in a bowl and whisk well to combine. Season with salt. Cover and refrigerate until ready to serve.

To make the fried tomatoes, heat enough oil for deep-frying in a deep-fryer or saucepan on a charcoal grill to 350°F (180°C).

Meanwhile, season the tomato slices on both sides with salt and pepper.

Combine the dry mix in a shallow bowl. In another shallow bowl, beat the eggs with the milk. Dredge the tomato through the flour mixture, then the egg wash, and finally coat well in another layer of the dry mix.

Working in batches, fry the tomato slices for 2 to 3 minutes, until lightly golden. Transfer to a plate lined with paper towels to drain.

Serve the fried green tomatoes on their own with the chipotle sauce, or assemble into buns with a good dollop of sauce, a few butter lettuce leaves and slices of chile.

Fried Eggplant Sliders

These cornmeal-battered and fried eggplant sliders are easy to whip up, and make a great starter for friends and family around the campground. Make extra eggplant patties to serve the next day with your eggs for breakfast.

Photo courtesy of THOR Industries.

2 eggplants, peeled and cut into ¼-inch-thick (5 mm) rounds

1 teaspoon sea salt

1 cup (250 ml) buttermilk

8 slices of white bread

¾ cup (150 g) self-rising flour

½ cup (70 g) self-rising cornmeal

½ teaspoon freshly ground black pepper

Vegetable oil, for shallow-frying

1 cucumber, peeled and thinly sliced

Jalapeño mayo

¼ cup (55 g) whole-egg mayonnaise

3 whole pickled jalapeños, finely chopped

Grated zest of 1 lemon

½ teaspoon sea salt

Light a fire and let it burn down for about an hour until you obtain a medium heat; set a grill grate over the fire. Alternatively, use a gas burner or your stovetop.

Sprinkle both sides of the eggplant slices with the salt. Place in a single layer on paper towels and set aside for 30 minutes. Rinse and pat dry. Transfer the eggplant slices to a large bowl, pour in the buttermilk and set aside to soak for about 30 minutes, making sure the eggplant is submerged.

Meanwhile, remove the crusts from the bread and discard (or feed them to the seagulls), and cut the bread into rounds the same size as the eggplant. Set aside.

To make the jalapeño mayo, combine all the ingredients in a bowl.

Place the flour, cornmeal and ground black pepper in a shallow bowl and toss to combine. Drain the eggplant slices and dredge both sides in the flour mixture.

Pour 1½ inches (4 cm) of vegetable oil into a large cast-iron frying pan and heat to 375°F (190°C) or until a cube of bread dropped into the oil browns in 10 seconds. Working in batches, add the eggplant slices and fry for 3 minutes on each side or until golden brown. Transfer the eggplant slices to paper towels to drain.

Arrange the eggplant on the bread rounds, top with a few slices of cucumber and a dollop of jalapeño mayo and enjoy the sunset.

Blackened Gator Tail

I was OBSESSED with trying to hunt a gator and the South has heaps of them! Alligator hunting season is open six weeks a year as long as you have a tag. I never got to actually dispatch a gator myself, but I did eat a lot of gator meat throughout the season. Hunting gator is quite the process, let me tell you, and although my friend Michael Harris and I ventured out once (it was quite the adventure), the alligators we caught were unfortunately too small to harvest.

I created this dish using some of the tail meat from a whopping 11-foot (3.3 m) gator landed on opening night. Gator tastes like chicken or fish, but it also has a fattiness to it. Bizarre but true, and in the South they love to fry it, so I thought I would take a classic Southern dish and turn it on its head with the golden gator meat.

1 pound (450 g) gator tail, cut into bite-sized cubes

⅓ cup (80 ml) grapeseed oil, plus extra for cooking if needed

2 teaspoons smoked paprika

⅓ cup (50 g) coconut sugar

½ bird's eye chile, finely chopped

1 teaspoon grated fresh ginger

1 teaspoon finely chopped fresh oregano leaves

1 teaspoon finely chopped fresh parsley leaves

Ghee, for cooking

Lemon wedges, to serve

Roasted garlic aioli

1 garlic bulb

½ cup (110 g) mayonnaise

Zest of 1 lemon, plus 1 teaspoon lemon juice

Sea salt, to taste

Light your fire and let it burn down for 1 hour until you obtain a medium heat.

Meanwhile, place all of the ingredients except the ghee and lemon wedges in a large bowl and mix well with your hands to coat the gator tail. Set aside to marinate for 1 hour.

To make the garlic aioli, wrap the garlic bulb in aluminum foil and place it in the coals of the fire. Cook for about 1 hour, until soft, then remove from the coals and allow to cool.

Place the mayonnaise in a small bowl, then squeeze the barbecued garlic bulb over the mayonnaise to release the soft roasted garlic cloves inside. Add the lemon zest and juice and salt to taste, and stir to combine. Set aside.

Melt a little ghee on a sear plate or drizzle with grapeseed oil. If you don't have a sear plate you can place a grill grate about 12 inches (30 cm) above the coals and use a cast-iron frying pan. Add the gator meat, along with the marinade, and cook, turning every minute or when the underside of the gator tail turns brown, for 5 minutes or until opaque in the middle and cooked through.

Serve with the garlic aioli on the side and lemon wedges.

Main
Feeds 4

Equipment: Breeo Fire Pit and
Sear plate • Cast-iron frying pan

Half-Shell Redfish

I gotta say, for me, food is an integral part of experiencing culture. I really wanted to learn more about fishing in the USA and about what species of animals I could hunt. Redfish are found along the inner coast of Florida. They have a similar flavor to snapper, and they're super fun to catch. Cooking on the half shell was a new experience for me — you simply leave the scales on when you remove the fillets from the fish. The scales act as a barrier between the fish and the fire and function as a frying pan. Genius!

½ cup (145 g) white miso paste

2 tablespoons sesame oil

1 tablespoon grated fresh turmeric or 1 teaspoon ground turmeric

1 tablespoon grated fresh ginger

4 garlic cloves, grated or finely diced

Handful of fresh cilantro (coriander) stalks, diced

4 redfish fillets, or any firm white fish fillets, scales and skin left on

Sauce of your choice, to serve

Salad of your choice, to serve

In a large bowl, combine the miso paste, sesame oil, turmeric, ginger, garlic and diced cilantro stalks and mix well to combine. Add the fish and turn to coat well in the marinade, then set aside in the fridge for a minimum of 2 hours.

An hour before you're ready to cook the fish, light a fire and let it burn down for about an hour until you obtain a medium heat, but still with hot coals. Place a grill grate about 8 inches (20 cm) above the coals.

Place the fish, skin-side down, on the grill and cook for 10 to 15 minutes, until the flesh is opaque and the scales are crisp.

Serve immediately off the grill, with your favorite sauces and a fresh salad on the side.

Oyster Roast

Believe it or not, Florida has INCREDIBLE oysters. Growing up in Tasmania, I assumed that only cold-water oysters were any good. Nope, Florida warm-water oysters are sweet, creamy and salty. It's so much fun to gather your friends, stand around a table, shuck oysters, drink beer and laugh your way through a bushel! It's very easy to harvest your own or simply find a local to sell you some.

100 to 120 unshucked oysters (about 1 bushel), scrubbed clean

Mignonette

½ cup (70 g) finely minced shallot

¼ cup (60 ml) white vinegar

¼ cup (60 ml) unseasoned rice vinegar (if using seasoned rice vinegar, omit the sugar and salt)

1/8 teaspoon sugar

1/8 teaspoon sea salt

1¼ teaspoons finely crushed white peppercorns (do not use pre-ground or powdered white pepper)

To serve

6 small lemons, cut into wedges

Tabasco sauce, or other hot pepper sauce

To make the mignonette, place the minced shallot in a non-reactive bowl. Add the white vinegar, rice vinegar, sugar, and salt and stir to combine with a fork. Add the crushed white peppercorns and stir again, then cover with plastic wrap and chill in the fridge for a minimum of 4 hours for the flavors to infuse.

Heat your Traeger grill to 475°F (250°C). Working in batches, arrange the oysters in a single layer in a 12 x 16 inch (30 x 40 cm) roasting pan fitted with a flat rack. Pour ⅛ inch (1 cm) of hot tap water into the pan, transfer the pan to the grill and roast the oysters for 7 minutes or until they just begin to open.

Using gloves or tongs, transfer the oysters to a table covered in newspaper and invite your guests to shuck the oysters, garnish with their choice of mignonette, lemon wedges or Tabasco, and eat while the next batch cooks, adding more water to the pan as necessary.

<u>Side</u>

Feeds a crowd

Equipment: Traeger pellet grill
(alternatively, use a charcoal
barbecue grill) • Roasting pan   2 1 1

Venison Schnitzel

You can use any meat for this recipe. I like venison, as it's always an underrated meat and it's readily available as an ethical source of meat — especially if you hunt. I also enjoy deconstructing this recipe by serving the cutlets (without the buns) topped with tomato sauce and cheese with a fresh salad on the side.

1–2 venison rump steaks, divided into 6 steaks

3 cups (300 g) fresh breadcrumbs

3 eggs

3 tablespoons chopped fresh flat-leaf parsley

1 tablespoon minced garlic

Salt and freshly ground black pepper

Ghee, for cooking

$\frac{1}{3}$ cup (75) mayonnaise, for spreading

6 brioche buns, split

6 slices tomato

6 lettuce leaves

Condiments of your choice, to serve

Light your fire and let it burn down for 1 hour until you obtain a medium heat.

Place a grill grate over the fire about 12 inches (30 cm) above the coals.

Place the venison on a sturdy surface, such as a tree log or a chopping board, and use a meat mallet or similar to pound and flatten the steaks to a thickness of $\frac{1}{8}$ inch (2 mm).

Spread the breadcrumbs on a tray or other flat surface. Lightly beat the eggs in a bowl, adding the parsley, garlic, 1 teaspoon salt and a good grinding of pepper. Submerge the venison in the egg mixture, thoroughly drenching both sides, then transfer to the breadcrumbs and press to coat on both sides.

Place a large cast-iron frying pan on the grill grate. Add a generous dollop of ghee and let it melt, then fry the schnitzels for 4 minutes on each side. Remove and drain on paper towels to ensure your schnitzels stay crisp.

Spread some mayonnaise on the insides of the buns and toast, mayo-side down, in the pan until golden brown.

Layer the venison schnitzels, tomato and lettuce on the buns, season with salt and finish with your choice of condiments.

Recipe created in collaboration with Breeo.

Main

Feeds 6

Equipment: Breeo Fire Pit and
Outpost Grill or grill grate
• Large cast-iron frying pan

2 1 5

Big Cookout (Steak Done Right)

Cooking steak on an open fire is a beautiful method to infuse your meat with the rich flavors of smoke. It's something that is often overlooked in cookbooks, so I wanted to talk about how to cook a great steak over the campfire.

The key to a good steak is patience, good quality meat (I used Cape Grim beef from Tasmania) and the right grill plate to cook it on. I'm using this super nifty grill plate that has an adjustable grate so I can move it around my fire easily.

The hardest thing about cooking on an open fire is that the wind can be unpredictable. To be honest, it's trial and error, but here are a few key tricks.

2 pounds (900 g) rib-eye steak

2 cups/4 sticks (440 g) salted butter

Sea salt flakes

Light your fire an hour before cooking on it — you want nice coals to cook over. Place the grill grate about 15 inches (38 cm) above the coals, so that the heat won't cook your meat fast, but it will get some warmth and smoke.

Get your meat out of the cooler and bring it to room temperature prior to cooking. You want good quality grass-fed meat — don't skimp on it, or it will be tough and the flavor will be like water.

Season the steak well with sea salt flakes. While the steak is coming to room temperature, put your butter in the pot on the grill grate; you want it low and slow so that the butter separates from the milk solids. The idea here is that you are making ghee, removing water from the butter, and leaving just the pure fat and great flavor. I use this a lot when cooking over open fire.

Smear some butter/ghee over the meat and place it on the grill grate to start smoking and infusing the flavor of the fire in it. We are trying to break down the fats in the meat so that it bastes with them while cooking.

<u>Main</u>

Feeds 6

Equipment: Breeo Fire Pit and
Outpost Grill or grill grate • Pot

Don't flip the steak or be tempted to lift it up. Leave the
meat over the coals for 20 minutes before flipping. Prior
to flipping, add more butter/ghee and salt. You're looking
for caramelization on the meat, without overcooking it.
You can use a meat thermometer to check for the right
temperature.

After flipping, keep cooking and basting in butter/ghee as
desired, until it reaches an internal temperature of 130-
135°F (55-60°C) for medium rare. Remove from the grill
and allow to rest for 10 minutes before slicing and serving
with your desired dressing.

Watermelon Salad

I have very fond memories of riding bikes around Florida in the blistering sun, sweating and wondering if we will ever get relief from this humidity? In those moments, you always pass a roadside stall busting with LARGE juicy watermelons. Most of the time we would just crack open that juicy melon to quench our thirst, other times we would chill it and make this salad married with greasy fried chicken. After a long day in the sun or at the beach you will be sleeping well this night!

½ cup (1-pound / 500 g) watermelon, cut into 1½-inch (4 cm) chunks, chilled

1 lime, juiced

½ cup (12.5 g) coarsely chopped fresh mint leaves

½ cup (30 g) coarsely chopped fresh flat-leaf parsley

2 teaspoons salt

½ teaspoon freshly ground black pepper

½ pound (230 g) feta cheese, crumbled

2 lime cheeks, for garnish

In a large bowl, add the watermelon and the lime juice and toss gently.

Add the mint, cilantro and parsley and toss. Sprinkle the jalapeño rings over the top and season with salt and pepper.

Garnish with the crumbled feta and lime cheeks.

Picnic Cake

Florida has been on my personal map for a long time now: I lived here for 8 months, and had the chance to spend some time with my dear friend Jill McCloghry and her family. It was such a sweet season for me! I loved our beach hangouts, and this picture makes me smile for so many reasons. We did a little girls' hang on the beach, and this very moment is what I live for. The choccy cake just made it a bit sweeter. Hehe.

4 ounces (125 g) dark chocolate

1 teaspoon rum or brandy

1 teaspoon hot black coffee

6 tablespoons plus 2 teaspoons (90 g) butter

½ cup (90 g) superfine (caster) sugar

1 cup (90 g) almond meal

3 eggs, separated

Cream, to serve

Light your fire and let it burn down for 1 hour until you obtain a medium heat. Set up your tripod.

Break the chocolate into small bits and drop into a medium pot. cook over the grill grate over the fire. Add the rum or brandy and coffee and allow to melt over the fire, stirring to combine. Add the butter, sugar and almond meal and stir over the fire until all ingredients are smooth and combined.

Meanwhile, beat the egg yolks well and, in a separate bowl, whip the egg whites until stiff peaks form.

Take the pot off the heat and stir in the beaten egg yolk, then gently fold in the whipped whites. Line your Dutch oven with parchment paper, then pour in the batter. Cover with the lid, then hang the pan off your tripod and shovel some coals on top (so it cooks both the top and the bottom). Cook for 30 minutes, then remove from the fire and remove the lid. Because the cake has no flour, it's quite fragile — it's best to let it cool in the Dutch oven before turning out, or just cut it in the Dutch oven. Serve with cream and coffee.

<u>Sweets</u>   Feeds all your mates   Equipment: Tripod •
Cast-iron Dutch oven • Hand mixer

Golden Syrup Dumplings

These light, scone-like dumplings are an Australian classic that I felt needed to be introduced to the USA. To me, the USA is all about multicultural diversity and, of course, new trends, so it feels fitting to include this "Down Under" dessert here. It's a great campfire recipe, but you can also make it on the stovetop. Golden syrup is a light molasses that has a nice caramel flavor; maple syrup is a good substitute.

1 cup (120 g) self-rising flour, plus extra for dusting

Pinch of sea salt

1 tablespoon plus 1 teaspoon (20 g) salted butter

1 large egg, lightly beaten

3 tablespoons milk

Heavy whipping cream, to serve

Golden sauce

½ cup (175 g) golden syrup

¼ cup (70 g) molasses

¾ cup (155 g) firmly packed brown sugar

2 tablespoons (30 g) unsalted butter

1⅔ cups (410 ml) water

Light your fire and let the coals burn down for about an hour until you have a slight flame. Set a grill grate 12 inches (30 cm) above the coals.

Sift the flour into a bowl and add the salt. Rub the butter into the flour until it resembles breadcrumbs, then add the beaten egg and stir to combine.

Gradually add the milk and mix until the dough just comes together and resembles a loose and sticky dough (do not overwork the dough). Set aside.

Combine the sauce ingredients in a Dutch oven. Bring to the boil over the fire, stirring to combine the ingredients, then move to a cooler part of the fire and allow the sauce to gently simmer.

Flour your hands and roll the dough into golf ball–sized balls, then transfer to a baking sheet lined with parchment paper.

Slip the dough balls off the parchment paper and into the syrup. Cover with the lid, shovel some coals on top, and cook for about 10 minutes or until the dumplings are light and fluffy.

If you are cooking on a stovetop, simply cover with the lid and cook for 3 minutes. Using a spoon, gently turn over the dumplings and continue to cook until light and fluffy.

Remove the dumplings using a slotted spoon, and serve with the remaining sauce and a jug of cream.

Yummo!

<u>Sweets</u>

Feeds 4

Equipment: Grill grate
• Cast-iron Dutch oven

CAMPGROUND APRÈS

THIS CALLS FOR A TOAST

All this traveling is thirsty work, right? I can fix that, but first, coffee.

There's nothing I love more than sitting in a chair at the dawn of a new day, enjoying a freshly brewed coffee while watching the sun rise. For those travelers who love a morning coffee, the routine around preparing it and the aroma it encompasses — you are my people. Of course, don't shy away from trying the regional brew wherever you land. One of the best ways to find community while you're on the road is to seek out the occasional cappuccino and bag of beans from the local coffee house.

Obviously, while you're on the road, storage space is prime real estate within your home on wheels, and a couple of hacks here might not go astray. Consider dehydrating your coffee before you embark on your adventure, so you can make instant coffee whenever the occasion arises. It also makes prep fuss-free if you can pre-grind your coffee (it'll also save you hand grinding at that moment when you really just need

a coffee). For those seeking the ultimate coffee experience, consider investing in the AeroPress and the Hario V60 for the best quality coffee. Oh, and make sure you use beans roasted for filter or drip coffee makers, rather than for espresso, as espresso is a darker roast — and you won't be able to taste the delicate flavors, like you would in a filter.

Ready for a sundowner? Let me just start by saying this next chapter is not about creating your average drink. We're going to forage for garnishes, add fire where we can, and create interesting mixers because, after all, we're on a wild adventure together! When it comes to creating the perfect cocktail I'd encourage you to find your inspiration wherever your road trip may lead you, to forage where possible and to match your cocktail to your surroundings — check out the Campfire Cactus if you're planning a Joshua Tree stint!

Above all else, have a little fun with it. You're on vacation!

Oyster Shooter

When I was traveling through the Napa Valley with some mates of mine, we landed at a spot that sold fresh oysters with a bottle of mezcal. No cups, just an epic view. So we ate the oyster and did a shot of mezcal, and proceeded to crow like a rooster? Ha. You can forgo the crowing part, but I highly recommend this combination. You could also try it with a crisp white wine. Why get fancy when you can just embrace the moment?

1 bottle of delicious mezcal

Dozen oysters (or more)

This is easy: you just need to shuck the oyster and then throw it back in your mouth, and follow it up with a shot of mezcal in the oyster shell.

<u>Drinks</u>

Feeds all your mates

Sarah's Margarita

A cold Margarita in the desert always goes down too easily. This is my way to drink it. I was never much of a Margarita drinker until exploring the USA — now I crave them. The slight spicy hit makes the hot summer days cooler.

1 lime wedge

Table salt for salted rim

2 jalapeño peppers, cored and seeds removed

2 ounces (60 ml) tequila

1 ounce (30 ml) orange liqueur

1 ounce (30 ml) freshly squeezed lime juice

½ ounce (15 ml) agave syrup

Rub the rim of a rocks glass with a lime wedge, dip the rim in salt to coat, and set aside.

If you have a fire going, you can add the jalapeño peppers to the grill and roast until blistered and charred in places, about 20 minutes. When cool enough to handle, slice the roasted jalapeños into rings and add 3 rings to a shaker; gently muddle.

Add the tequila, orange liqueur, lime juice and agave syrup to the shaker, plus ice, and shake until well chilled. Strain into the prepared glass over fresh ice.

Makes 1

Coconut Holiday

For me, being on a road trip feels like a tropical holiday. I grew up on an island that was cold, so whenever I went on holiday it was to someplace warm and it always involved fresh coconuts. I thought it was appropriate to have an option for those who want a taste of a tropical holiday. Coconut at sunset? Yes, please.

Mezcal (for a rinse)

2 ounces (60 ml) light rum

1½ ounces (45 ml) coconut cream

5 fresh cilantro (coriander) leaves, plus more for garnish, optional

1 small fresh chile, for garnish (such as Thai)

Rinse a serving glass with mezcal. Fill the glass with ice (preferably crushed but cubed will work just fine).

Add all the remaining ingredients except the fresh chile to a cocktail shaker, add ice, and shake vigorously for 10 to 15 seconds. Strain into the ice-filled serving glass (add more ice to make a half dome).

Garnish with a Thai pepper or cilantro. (If you have a fire going, roast the pepper prior to garnishing.)

Drinks   Makes 1

Sweet Daisy

Gin is a go-to for me when road tripping — it's light and easy to drink (and a good G & T never fails). With this version, I prettied up this classic drink a little. It's not too sweet, but has a fresh summer feeling to it. Why not try to find some edible flowers to garnish your drink with?

2 ounces (60 ml) gin

1 ounce (30 ml) freshly squeezed lime juice

2 ounces (60 ml) Hibiscus Syrup (recipe below)

3 strawberries, chopped, plus more for garnish

Dash of tonic water

Edible flowers, for garnish

Fill cocktail shaker with gin, lime juice, hibiscus syrup, and fresh strawberries.

Shake mixture and then double strain into the serving glass.

Hibiscus Syrup

2 cups (60 g) dried Jamaica flowers, also known as hibiscus or flor de Jamaica

4 cups (1 L) water

1 cup (225 g) sugar

Makes 2 cups (600 ml)

In a large pot, place the 2 cups (80 g) of dried Jamaica and add 4 cups (1 L) water.

Over medium-high heat, bring to a soft boil for 5 minutes. Remove from the heat.

Add the sugar and stir well until all of the sugar is dissolved.

I let mine sit overnight covered on my counter because I like it to have a strong flavor!

Makes 1

Fireside Hot Toddy

This is a good jet lag cure, if you're traveling through time zones. I like to think of it as more of an elixir, minus the booze.

¾ cup (180 ml) water

3 teaspoons raw honey, plus more to taste

2 teaspoons freshly squeezed lemon juice, plus more to taste

1 chamomile tea bag

1 teaspoon of equal parts cinnamon, nutmeg and cardamom spice blend

1½ ounces (45 ml) bourbon

1 ounce (30 ml) Grand Marnier

1 lemon round, for garnish (optional)

Cinnamon stick, for garnish (optional)

In a teapot or saucepan, bring the water to a simmer. Add the honey, lemon juice, spice blend and chamomile tea bag and continue to simmer for 3 minutes. Discard the chamomile tea bag and pour the hot water mixture into a mug. Add the bourbon and Grand Marnier. Taste, and add 1 teaspoon honey for more sweetness, and/or 1 teaspoon lemon juice for more zing. Garnish with a lemon round and cinnamon stick, if using. Enjoy!

Makes 1

Sunset Drive

Sunsets by the coast in California are always so dreamy, and the light turns a hazy pink as it drops over the sea. I know it's kind of ridiculous to take Champagne coupes with you on the road, but cruising Malibu at sunset with Peggy North in her dreamy cars made for an even more magical moment with a fancy drink in hand that matched the sky.

1 cup (250 ml) water

1 cup (225 g) sugar

6 strawberries

Handful of fresh basil leaves, plus extra for garnish

1 lime

4 ounces (120 ml) rum

Club soda

In a small saucepan, mix together the water and sugar. Bring the mix to a boil over medium heat. Let the sugar syrup cool for 15 to 20 minutes.

Divide the strawberries between two tall glasses and add some crushed basil leaves to each. Crush (muddle) the strawberries with a fork or spoon.

Cut the lime in half and slice two slices from the middle. Add one to each glass. Juice the remaining lime and divide between the two glasses.

Add about ¼ cup (60 ml) of the sugar syrup (you will have extra) to each glass and then half the rum in each glass. Stir to blend well.

Fill each glass with ice and top with club soda to taste. Garnish with more basil.

Drinks   Makes 2

Californian Light

This recipe is perfect for traveling, as you can prepare the mixer at home and take it with you on the road. Making your own mixtures is a fun option worth exploring. You'll be surprised at how man fruits can be dehydrated! It makes for light travel and your ingredients don't go off while on the road. All you have to do is add some water to the jar of dehydrated ingredients, wait a few hours for it to infuse (like a tea) and you're good to go.

1 mandarin orange, sliced into 5 disks

1 blood orange, sliced into 5 disks

½ vanilla bean

5 sugar cubes

2 ounces (60 ml) Desert Door Original Texas Sotol

Fresh cilantro (coriander), optional

Dehydrate the mandarin and blood orange disks at 140° F (60° C) for 6 hours. Reserve 2 citrus disks for garnish. Add the remaining dehydrated fruit to a clean jar with the vanilla bean and sugar. Keep this ready for the adventure. When you're ready to make the drink, simply add 1 cup (250 ml) of boiling water to the jar and let it steep for 3 hours or up to 24 hours.

To serve, place some ice in your cocktail shaker. Add the sotol, along with 4 ounces (120 ml) of the mixer and a sprig of fresh cilantro. Shake, pour over ice in a cup, and garnish each drink with a citrus disk.

Campfire Cactus

This drink reminds me of crisp desert nights. It's cool and refreshing, perfectly paired with a smoky, warm fire. I spent some time in Texas doing a wild feast with Desert Door in Austin at the end of spring, so I wanted to create a drink that reminded me of that moment under the stars with a field full of friends and the sound of a howling coyote in the distance.

3 pineapple rings

2 limes, halved

2 ounces (60 ml) Desert Door Original Texas Sotol

½ ounce (15 ml) agave nectar

Chili-lime salt, such as Tajín

Light your fire and let the coals burn down for about an hour until you have a slight flame. Set a grill grate 12 inches (30 cm) above the coals. Add the pineapple rings and lime halves, (cut-side down) to the grill. Flip once and cook until charred (about 10 minutes). Rim an old-fashioned glass with a lime half and coat with the chili-lime salt. Muddle the pineapple in a shaker. Squeeze 3 lime halves into the shaker and add the sotol, agave nectar and ice. Shake vigorously. Strain the cocktail into the prepared glass over fresh ice.

THANK YOU

Pulling this book together has been quite the ride. Every twist, turn and bend in the road has made this an incredible experience all round. From nostalgia to utter awe, this journey has challenged my emotions and my understanding of this country, and inspired an appreciation in me that in all honesty, has left me wanting more of this place.

America, as to be expected, you did not disappoint, and I am so happy to have had the opportunity to share parts of this glorious country with a community of travelers who are eager to see some of what this country has to offer. While we didn't make it to every state, those places we did visit were as awe-inspiring as I could have imagined, providing the ultimate backdrop for some really great cooking experiences.

Of course, a book like this is a team effort, and there are a number of people I need to thank for their time, dedication and united vision, because without that, this Wild American Road Trip wouldn't be here.

Thanks to:

Prestel Publishing. I'm so thankful to have such a wonderful publisher supporting my career and outdoor adventures! Here's to many more road trips.

My Sponsors. As you can imagine embarking upon a journey like this, I wanted to ensure readers had access to some of my favorite brands, so you could see them put to use. Big thanks to Thor Motor Coach®, Dometic, Front Runner, Gozney, Breeo, Outdoorsy, Autocamp, Commercial Dehydrators, Greenham, Barebones and Kodiak Cakes.

Katrina Parker. My dear friend, we met when we both took a leap of faith towards our careers. I'm so thankful for all your hard work and dedication to this project and for supporting me in my career. And to Dave, thank you for holding it down on the family front while we were gallivanting around America.

Holly McCauley. Creating with you is just so fun and easy. Thanks for always bringing your style and flair to my books and helping my work come to life. Three books down!

Felicity Bonello and Ariella Werner-Seidler. Thank you for being my Girl Band team, for supporting me and helping me to share my voice.

Dylan Handley, Kaitlin Harris, Mallory Aussem and Lauren Pandolfi. I'm so grateful for your creativity on this project, as contributing photographers.

Susan, Dez, Isabeaux, Simone. Your support over the years has made these pages all the more meaningful and full of authenticity. Much love, forever.

Vincent Grupposo. The original American who opened my eyes to more than hot dogs and Toyota Camrys, our friendship has propelled my creativity. I'm so thankful for your heart. Here is to many more years side by side, this book is dedicated to you. Love.

Dad and Mum Glover and my family. I am always so grateful for your heart.

Matt, Jill, Mazey Jack, and Charlie McCloghry. You and your family have impacted me immensely. I will never forget your kindness and your genuine care and love in seeing me thrive. Love you. #family.

St. Augustine friends. Thank you for being a pivotal part in my journey, and welcoming me back to the fair land. You know who you all are, life in community is the only life for me.

California family. Thank you for welcoming me to your shores and allowing me to surf and create.

Travelers on the road. I'm so thankful for this community and so grateful we have each other.

INDEX

248

C

INDEX

INDEX

© Prestel Verlag, Munich · London · New York, 2023
A member of Penguin Random House Verlagsgruppe GmbH
Neumarkter Strasse 28 · 81673 Munich

©Photography: Kat Parker
© Text and recipes: Sarah Glover
With contributions from:
Kaitlin Harris
Dylan Handley
Kotryna Liepinyte, Courtesy of Kodiak Cakes
HB Mertz, Courtesy of Breeo

Library of Congress Control Number is available;
a CIP catalogue record for this book is available from
the British Library.

In respect to links in the book, the Publisher expressly notes
that no illegal content was discernible on the linked sites at the
time the links were created. The Publisher has no influence at all over
the current and future design, content or authorship of the linked sites.
For this reason the Publisher expressly disassociates itself from all
content on linked sites that has been altered since the link was created
and assumes no liability for such content.

Editorial direction: Claudia Stäuble
Project management: Veronika Brandt
Copyediting: Monica Parcell
Design and layout: Holly McCauley
Production management: Luisa Klose
Separations: Reproline mediateam
Printing and binding: Livonia Print, Riga
Paper: Amber Graphic

Penguin Random House Verlagsgruppe FSC® N001967

Printed in Latvia

ISBN 978-3-7913-8944-8

www.prestel.com